365 ODDBALL DAYS

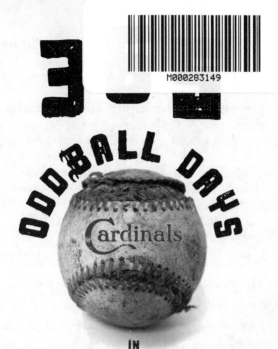

Cardinals

IN
ST. LOUIS CARDINALS HISTORY

JOHN SNYDER

CLERISY PRESS

365 Oddball Days in St. Louis Cardinals History

For further information, contact the publisher at:

Clerisy Press
P.O. Box 8874
Cincinnati, OH 45208-0874
www.clerisypress.com

Library of Congress Cataloging-in-Publication Data

Snyder, John.
  365 oddball days in St. Louis Cardinals history / by John Snyder.
    p. cm.
  ISBN-13: 978-1-57860-471-5
  ISBN-10: 1-57860-471-0
  1. St. Louis Cardinals (Baseball team)—History. 2. St. Louis Cardinals
    (Baseball team)—Miscellanea. I. Title. II. Title: Three hundred
    sixty five oddball days in St. Louis Cardinals history.
  GV875.S74C366 2011
  796.357'640977866—dc22
                                    2011008915

Edited by Jack Heffron
Cover designed by Stephen Sullivan
Interior designed by Scott McGrew
Distributed by Publishers Group West

About the Author

John Snyder has a master's degree in history from the University of Cincinnati and a passion for baseball. He has authored more than fifteen books on baseball, soccer, hockey, tennis, football, basketball and travel. He lives in Cincinnati.

Welcome to the Oddball Series, Cardinals fans.

Here you'll find a wide assortment of the oddest players and moments—wild, weird, wacky, sometimes even wonderful—in team history. In fact, you'll find one for every day of the year.

Not just a round-up of the stories that have been told over and over, this Oddball history by SABR Research Award–winning author John Snyder digs deep into Cardinals history to give you a daily dose of fresh tales you probably haven't heard before.

Each page brings you something new—whether it's "happy birthday" to a colorful Cardinal or an "on this day" slice of history, or a question that only the most serious diehards will be able to answer.

Take, for example, May 30, 1922, when the Cardinals traded Cliff Heathcoat to the Cubs for Max Flack in between games of a doubleheader in Chicago. The players walked to the formerly opposing locker rooms and put on new uniforms to play against guys who had been their teammates just minutes ago.

Or the sad tale of Tommy Glaviano, a Cardinals third baseman who helped blow an 8-0 lead on May 13, 1950, by committing four errors, three of them in the ninth inning on three consecutive plays.

Though 13 wasn't Tommy's lucky number, it seemed even worse for pitcher Mort Cooper, who normally wore it on his uniform. But in 1942 he'd been trying for more than a month to win his 14th game. To change his luck, he changed his uniform, putting on Gus Mancuso's number 14 for a game on August 14. He won 4-0 on a two-hitter. For the rest of the season, Cooper wore a uniform number that corresponded to the victory total he was seeking. He won seven games in seven consecutive starts, finishing the year by winning the National League Most Valuable Player Award with a 22-7 record.

And then there's September 7, 1993, when "Hard Hittin'" Mark Whiten produced 14 runs in a single game by hitting four homers and knocking in 12 against the Reds. He produced the other two runs by committing an error that allowed the Reds to score twice.

Enjoy *365 Oddball Days in St. Louis Cardinals History.* You'll laugh, cheer, and learn a whole lot of stories that will make you the hit of the next long rain delay.

Jack Heffron, series editor

January

Cardinals

01
January

The question of the day: When did the St. Louis Cardinals begin?

The present-day Cardinals have been part of the National League since 1892 but have their roots in the American Association, where the club played from 1882 through 1891. The official beginning of the franchise dates from November 2, 1881, with the creation of the American Association in a meeting held in Cincinnati. But the foundations of the franchise that would become the Cardinals extend even a few years earlier. The 1869 Cincinnati Red Stockings, baseball's first professional club, toured the country and made two visits to St. Louis, playing local amateur teams. In September 1869, the Red Stockings defeated the Unions 70-9 and the Empires 31-9. The Empires were managed by Jeremiah Fruin, a young man from Brooklyn who was posted in St. Louis during the Civil War while serving in the Union Army's Quartermaster Corps. Brooklyn was a hotbed of baseball, and Fruin learned the game as a youngster. He remained in St. Louis after the war ended and taught the sport to many people, inspiring so much interest that a professional team was inevitable. Though he later protested the nickname, Fruin became known as the "father of baseball in St. Louis." He later became a successful businessman and for a time served as the city's Police Commissioner.

02 January

The question of the day: What were the first St. Louis teams in an organized league?

Baseball's first organized league was the National Association, formed in 1871. Two St. Louis clubs joined the NA in 1875. The St. Louis Red Stockings played on a lot bounded by Compton Avenue, Gratiot Street, railroad tracks, Theresa Avenue and Scott Street. The Brown Stockings used the site at Grand and Dozier, which acquired the name Sportsman's Park. At the end of the 1875 season, both the Red Stockings and the National Association folded. The Brown Stockings joined the National League, established in 1876, but dropped out after the 1877 season, leaving the city without a major league club.

03
January

The question of the day: How did the founder of *The Sporting News* help revitalize baseball after the demise of the Brown Stockings in 1877?

Al Spink, who later founded *The Sporting News* in 1886, formed the Sportsman's Park and Club Association following the demise of the Brown Stockings. The first task of Spink's group was to put Sportsman's Park into playing shape. Then they assembled a team and began to book exhibition games against the best opposition available. The primary investor in the association was Chris Von der Ahe, an ambitious entrepreneur who owned a boarding house and saloon near the site. Von der Ahe knew next to nothing about baseball, but he did know that business increased every time a baseball game took place at Grand and Dozier. Von der Ahe steered the club into the American Association and adopted the nickname Brown Stockings, later shortened to Browns. The nickname Browns passed out of use after Von der Ahe sold the franchise in 1899. The Cardinals nickname became attached to the team in 1900.

Cardinals

04 January

The question of the day: Why are they called the Cardinals?

For the sake of simplicity, St. Louis's National League baseball team is called the "Cardinals" throughout this book, but the franchise was called the Browns from the time it joined the American Association in 1882 until the end of the 1898 season. Frank and Stanley Robison bought the club prior to the 1899 season and changed the predominant color on the uniforms from brown to vivid red. The nickname Browns was no longer appropriate, and local sportswriters began referring to the club as the "Perfectos." According to legend, Willie McHale, a reporter for the *St. Louis Republic,* overheard a female fan remark, "What a lovely shade of cardinal" after seeing the club's red uniforms early in the 1900 season. McHale began using the nickname "Cardinals" in his articles, and it gradually moved into general use. This was typical of the period. Many team names were created not by the clubs, but by sportswriters. Clubs of the period were often called the name of the city, such as the "Chicagos" or "New Yorks." The name "Browns" gained new life in 1902 when the American League moved the Milwaukee franchise to St. Louis and called it the Browns, who existed until 1953, when the team moved to Baltimore and was renamed the Orioles.

Cardinals

05
January

The Cardinals signed free agent Matt Holliday on this date in 2010. It wasn't an oddball day—or even surprising—when the Cards signed Holliday, who played sixty-three games for the team in 2009 after a mid-season trade. The size and length of the contract—seven years and $120 million—did surprise some fans, who worried that such a big commitment would hinder the team's ability to sign mega-star Albert Pujols. Holliday had helped the team make the playoffs in 2009, but some fans could not forgive his goof in game two of the first-round series against the Los Angeles Dodgers. The Cardinals were leading 2-1 with two outs in the ninth inning with the bases empty when James Loney hit a line drive right to Holliday for what should have been an easy final out, but Holliday lost sight of the ball, which slammed into his belly and bounced onto the field. Loney ended up on second base and later scored to tie the game, which the Dodgers went on to win. They then took game three to win the series. Despite his fine play that season in the field and with the bat, Holliday was best remembered that off season for the flub that blew the team's chances to win the pennant.

Cardinals

06
January

Today's trivia: When did the word "Cardinals" first appear on the team uniforms?

The Cardinals nickname didn't appear on the club's uniforms until 1918. Prior to that, the team was identified on the jerseys with the name of the city or with the interlocking capital "S," lower case "t" and capital "L" now familiar to Cardinal fans. The intertwining letters were a part of the team caps as early as 1900. The 1922 season was the first appearance on the club's uniforms of the unique graphic symbol featuring two redbirds perched on a sloping bat that passed through the letter "C" in the word Cardinals. It was included that season on both the home and road jerseys. The design motif has been included on the Cardinals' uniforms to this day, with the exception of a one-year absence in 1956. The public outcry over the elimination of the symbol led to its return in 1957.

07
January

Happy Birthday, Johnny Mize. "The Big Cat" was born on this date in 1913. Mize, a Hall of Famer, played for the Cardinals from 1936 through 1941 and twice led the NL in home runs during that period. He hit three homers in a strange game on May 13, 1940, that ended in an 8-8 tie against the Reds in Cincinnati. Mize homered in the second and third innings and again in the thirteenth. The third homer gave the Cards an 8-7 lead, but the Reds came back in their half. The game was then called because of darkness even though Crosley Field had lights. At the time, league rules prevented lights from being used to finish day games. Another twist: It was a make-up game due to a postponement in April, and the league neglected to assign umpires. Fortunately, NL umpire Larry Goetz lived in Cincinnati and was at home on a day off. The game was delayed for twenty-nine minutes until Goetz arrived. Reds coach Jimmie Wilson umpired at first base and Cardinals pitcher Lon Warneke was stationed at third. They were each paid fifty dollars by the league office for their service. Warneke became an umpire after his playing days ended, serving the NL from 1949 through 1955.

Cardinals

08
January

Today's trivia: The exact origin of the term "fan" to describe the enthusiastic supporter of a sport or a performing art is open for debate, but many sources claim it was first used to describe baseball devotees in St. Louis in 1883. Up until then, baseball fans were most commonly called "cranks" or "fanatics." Some say that Cardinals manager Ted Sullivan first used the expression "fan" as a short version of "fanatic." Others say it came from owner Chris Von der Ahe, who had difficulty pronouncing the word "fanatic" with his thick German accent.

09
January

The question of the day: Who were the St. Louis Maroons?

The St. Louis Maroons were part of an eight-team major league started in 1884 to compete with the National League and American Association. The chief backer of the Union Association was 26-year-old Henry Lucas, whose family had large real estate holdings and owned several trolley car lines. He built Union Grounds for his club at the southeast corner of Cass and Jefferson. The park had a capacity of 10,000 and included upholstered folding opera chairs and leisure facilities. A cage of canaries serenaded patrons entering the park. With such amenities, it was dubbed "The Palace Park of America." Lucas set about to build a strong team, but it might have been *too* good as it destroyed the pennant race—and the interest of fans in many of the league's seven other cities. The Maroons won their first 20 games and finished the season with a record of 94-19. The UA also hoped to lure top players away from the NL and AA but generally failed as most major leaguers chose to remain in the two established leagues rather than risk their future in an untested organization.

Cardinals

10
January

On this date in Cardinals history, coach Joe Schultz died in 1996 in St. Louis at age 77. He grew up in St. Louis, the son of Joe Sr., a former MLB player who later managed the Cardinals formidable farm system built by Branch Rickey. Joe Jr. played nine seasons in the majors, for the Pirates and for the Browns. After retirement, he became a minor league coach, coming to the Cardinals organization in 1958. He made it to the big club in 1963 and coached for the Cardinals through the 1968 season. Then in 1969 he was hired to manage the first-year expansion Seattle Pilots. And that's where he found a certain national fame or, more accurately, notoriety, with the publication of Jim Bouton's classic baseball book, *Ball Four*. In the book, Joe is portrayed as overwhelmed by the challenge of creating a team from scratch, a task he confronts mostly through cryptic advice and creative cursing. He not only curses a lot, he even invents new curse words. He was fired after one year as the Pilots' pilot but moved on to coach through 1976 in the majors, having patiently suffered through his 15 minutes of fame.

Cardinals

11
January

On this date in 1968, the Cardinals traded outfielder Alex Johnson to Cincinnati in exchange for outfielder Dick Simpson. One of the most difficult players in the history of the franchise—maybe even the league—Alex Johnson was a gifted hitter who was chronically unhappy. Though he was already seen as a malcontent during his first years with the Phillies, his talent was enticing enough for the Cardinals, in October 1965, to trade respected veterans Bill White, Dick Groat and Bob Uecker for Johnson and two lesser players. Johnson's rare combination of speed and power showed promise of stardom. Unfortunately, "AJ" showed little interest in reaching his potential and soon found himself in the minors. When he was with the big club, he was often chided and even fined for lackadaisical play. When told to shift position in the outfield he ignored coaches and fellow players. He sulked on the bench. He even fought teammate Bobby Tolan. After two years of frustration, the Cardinals, as would every other team Johnson played for, gave up and traded him. Simpson managed only 65 plate appearances for the Cards and was shipped out after the season.

Cardinals

12 January

The question of the day: When was the Cardinals' radio network established?

The Cardinals set up a radio network consisting of out-of-town stations for the first time in 1938. Games that season were aired on stations in Columbia and Jefferson City in Missouri; Lincoln, Nebraska; Terre Haute, Indiana; Cedar Rapids, Des Moines and Shenandoah in Iowa; Yankton, South Dakota; and Jonesboro, Arkansas. The far-flung radio network would help transform the Cardinals into a regional franchise and boost attendance by inducing fans to travel hundreds of miles to see the team play in person. In 2010, the network included 36 stations in Missouri, 32 in Illinois, 13 in Arkansas, nine in Iowa, nine in Kentucky, six in Tennessee, three in Indiana, and one in Mississippi. The farthest station from St. Louis carrying Cardinals games is in Norman, Oklahoma, a distance of 463 miles.

Cardinals

13

January

On this date in 1920, Sam Breadon was elected president of the Cardinals. The club was in disarray, and Breadon proved to be the much-needed financial angel. He served as club president until 1947, during which the franchise won nine NL pennants and six World Series. The son of Irish immigrants, Breadon left New York City in 1902 at 26 to move to St. Louis with plans to open a garage and an automobile agency. He started as a mechanic in the fledgling industry, but was fired after only a few months. To make ends meet, he sold popcorn at the 1904 World's Fair, where he met Marion Lambert, a member of a prominent St. Louis family that owned a pharmaceutical company that marketed Listerine. Impressed by Breadon's plans for the future, Lambert offered him a partnership in the Western Automobile Company. The company made Breadon, a man with only a grade school education, a millionaire. He was one of 1,200 individuals who bought shares in the Cardinals in 1917 under a plan to make the club a community-owned affair. Breadon had little interest in baseball and initially owned only four shares, which he purchased for $2,000, but he became consumed by the sport and soon began buying more stock until he became majority owner in 1922. He sold the Cardinals in 1947 for $3 million and died in 1949.

14 January

Happy birthday, Paddy Livingston, who was born on this date in 1880. He played less than one season for the Cardinals—1917, his last one in the majors—and appeared in only seven games. He played only seven major league seasons, appearing in 205 games, but his professional career spanned 23 seasons, mostly in the minor leagues. A catcher, Paddy was a colorful, likable character who was a September call-up for the Cleveland Blues in 1901, the American League's first season. He played in one game, in which he appeared three times at the plate—against the legendary Cy Young. Though he was quickly retired twice, he did manage to get hit by a pitch. He would not appear again in a major league game until 1906. But when he died, on September 19, 1977, at the age of 97, he was the last living player from that first AL season.

Cardinals

15
January

The question of the day: Why did Cardinals owner Chris Von der Ahe have pitcher Mark Baldwin arrested?

In the fall of 1890, the National League and American Association clubs began claiming refugees from the Players League, which folded after one year. Baldwin signed with Pittsburgh and tried to persuade pitcher Silver King, one of the best in baseball, to join him. King pitched for the Cards before jumping to the Players League. When Von der Ahe discovered the scheme, he had Baldwin arrested for conspiracy, but the case was thrown out of court. As Baldwin left the courtroom, Von der Ahe had him arrested on new charges. Baldwin filed a $20,000 lawsuit against Von der Ahe for false arrest and malicious prosecution. The case was still not resolved on May 5, 1894, when Von der Ahe went to Pittsburgh, where he was arrested on a warrant issued at Baldwin's request. The jury awarded Baldwin $2,500. Unable to collect the money, Baldwin sued Von der Ahe again and was awarded $10,000 in 1897, but Von der Ahe refused to pay. So in February 1898, Baldwin had Von der Ahe kidnapped and forced onto a train for Pittsburgh, where he spent several days in jail but still wouldn't pay. Because the Pennsylvania court could not seize money Von der Ahe held in Missouri, Baldwin collected a portion of it by claiming a percentage of gate receipts when the Cards played in Pennsylvania.

Cardinals

16
January

On this date, two all-time great Cardinals were born. Happy birthday, Albert Pujols and Dizzy Dean. Pujols was born in 1980. He has been the team's superstar since he won the Rookie of the Year Award in 2001. Since then he has won three MVP awards and been selected nine times to the National League All-Star team. José Alberto Pujols Alcántara was born and raised in Santo Domingo, in the Dominican Republic. He moved to the U.S. in 1996 with his family, which settled in Independence, Missouri. Though he starred for his high school baseball team, he was not drafted. After he played for a year at Maple Woods Community College in Independence, the Cardinals drafted him in 1999 in the 13th round. From this humble start, Pujols quickly became a major league star and one of the most feared hitters in the game today. Jay Hanna "Dizzy" Dean was born in 1910 in Lucas, Arkansas. He came up with the Cards briefly in 1930 and then pitched for the team from 1932 through 1937. He was National League MVP in 1934, when he was the last pitcher in the league to win 30 games. He called Cards games on the radio from 1941 through 1946, becoming a beloved figure whose fracturing of the English language—using words like "slud" for "slid" and "swang" for "swung"— delighted fans.

17
January

On the date in 2004, the official groundbreaking ceremony was held to launch construction of the new Busch Stadium, which the Cardinals officially opened on April 10, 2006, with a game against the Milwaukee Brewers. The ballpark is the third to carry the Busch name. In 1953, the old Sportsman's Park was renamed Busch Stadium in honor the team's owner, August Busch. Following a national trend toward multi-purpose stadiums, St. Louis opened Busch Memorial Stadium in 1966. By the 1990s, the trend had shifted to baseball-only parks with more character than the circular, cookie-cutter buildings of the '60s and '70s. Teams also wanted to add to their coffers by adding luxury boxes and special seating. Early in the discussions with the city, the plan was to locate the park downtown, near the current stadium, but as often happens, discussions became arguments and soon there was talk of building the new Busch across the Mississippi River in Illinois. Many fans were outraged by the notion. Finally, state officials interceded and the park found a home next to the old one. In keeping with local tradition, the new ballpark would carry the name Cardinals fans had known for 50 years.

Cardinals

18
January

Today's trivia: What was extraordinary about John's Tudor's 1985 season?

The Cardinals acquired John Tudor from the Pirates along with Brian Harper in exchange for George Hendrick and Steve Bernard on December 12, 1984. Tudor had a 1-7 record on May 30, 1985, which drooped his career record to 52-50. A high school friend who had been following Tudor on cable television noticed the Cardinals hurler wasn't freezing his front leg long enough before delivering the ball to the plate, thus causing the leg to arrive long before his arm released the ball. Tudor corrected the problem, and over the remainder of the regular season, he won 20 of 21 decisions to finish the year with a 21-8 record and a 1.93 earned run average in 275 innings. Tudor also led the NL in shutouts with ten. The only Cardinals pitcher in the modern era with more shutouts is Bob Gibson with 13 in 1968. While posting the 20-1 record after May 30, Tudor's ERA was a remarkable 1.37. It was the only season in which Tudor won more than 13 games. He was 117-72 during his major league career, and 62-24 as a Cardinal from 1985 through 1988 and again in 1990.

Cardinals

19
January

Tommy Glaviano died on this date in 2004. As a Cardinal third baseman on May 13, 1950, Glaviano made four errors, three of them in the ninth inning on balls struck by three consecutive batters, which led to a 9-8 loss to the Dodgers at Ebbets Field. The Cardinals led 8-0 before Brooklyn scored four runs in the eighth inning. With a light rain falling on a cold night, the Dodgers scored one run and filled the sacks in the ninth with one out to set the stage for Glaviano's debacle. First he threw wide to second trying for a force play on Roy Campanella's grounder, allowing a run to score to make the tally 8-6. Glaviano then pegged wide to the plate on Eddie Miksis's grounder to allow another run to cross the plate while leaving the bases full. When Glaviano let Pee Wee Reese's hopper go through his legs, the tying and winning runs scored. That night, Enos Slaughter and coach Terry Moore took the despondent Glaviano to a movie at a Manhattan theater. The movie was *D.O.A.*, the story of a man attempting to find out who had given him a deadly, slow-acting poison. During spring training in 1951, the Cards tried Glaviano in center field. The first time he played the position in an exhibition contest, he crashed into the wall in the second inning and fell to the ground unconscious.

Cardinals

20 January

Happy Birthday, Tony Mullane. He was born on this date in 1859 in Ireland. He immigrated to the United States as a boy and pitched for eight teams from 1881 through 1894 with a won-lost ledger of 284-220. Mullane played for the Cardinals only in 1883, but made quite an impression with his 35-15 record, along with matinee-idol looks and flamboyant mustache, which made him a favorite of female fans. The *Cincinnati Enquirer* once observed that Mullane possessed an "arm like a freight car axle and calves that would have wooed the daughter of the Capulets away from Romeo." In his first five years in the majors, he played for five different clubs, infuriating owners by jumping his contract. Mullane played for Louisville in 1882 but refused to sign a contract and joined the Cardinals in 1883 for one year. When that deal expired, Mullane signed contracts with both Toledo of the American Association and St. Louis of the Union Association during the 1883-84 off-season. Mullane played for Toledo in 1884, but the franchise folded after the season ended. The Cardinals bought his contract, but Mullane signed with the Cincinnati Reds. He was suspended for the entire 1885 season, but was allowed to play for Cincinnati in 1886.

Cardinals

21
January

The question of the day: When did Cardinals players pose as carpenters at a hotel?

During the club's stay in Philadelphia in May 1936, Pepper Martin, Dizzy Dean and Heinie Schuble pulled a prank at the Bellevue-Stratford Hotel. Wearing overalls and long-peaked caps and carrying ladders and hammers, the three posed as carpenters. They first visited the banquet room, where about 200 people were attending a Rotary luncheon, and went about inspecting the place for repairs by moving tables and unseating many of Philadelphia's leading citizens. After those attending the banquet learned the identity of the "carpenters," the three ballplayers were invited to join the head table. Later, Martin, Dean and Schuble visited several other parts of the hotel, going through the same antics, finally invading a meeting of the United Boys' Club of America, where they got into a mock disagreement, and Dean bashed Martin to the floor with a resounding crack of his open hand. Cardinals management took a dim view of the shenanigans, however, which squashed a repeat performance.

Cardinals

22 January

On this date in 1945, Stan Musial was drafted and chose to enter military service with the Navy. Musial starred on the 1942, 1943 and 1944 Cardinals teams that won the National League pennant. The loss of Musial and others who were in the service—including Enos Slaughter, Walker Cooper, Howie Pollet, Murry Dickson, Johnny Beazley, Al Brazle, George Munger, Terry Moore, Erv Dusak, Lou Klein, Harry Walker and Ernie White—proved too much for the Cardinals to overcome. The Cardinals started the season with a 10-12 record before edging toward the top of the National League. The club stayed on the heels of the first-place Cubs until the last week of the season but couldn't close the gap and finished three games behind Chicago. The Cubs had fewer significant losses due to military commitments than any other NL team during World War II. If both the Cardinals and Cubs had been at full-strength in 1945, the Cardinals would have easily finished first. Had the Cards won the 1945 pennant, they would have been NL champions five years in a row, combined with victories in 1942, 1943, 1944 and 1946.

Cardinals

23
January

On this date in 1967, Bob Howsam resigned as general manager of the Cardinals to take a similar position with the Reds. Howsam took over as St. Louis general manager in August 1964. He had previously operated the minor league club in Denver from 1949 through 1961, and he was the original owner of the Denver Broncos in 1960, although he sold the club a year later. The Cardinals won the NL pennant in 1964, but after they sank to seventh in a ten-team league in 1965 and sixth in 1966 Howsam dealt long-time favorites like Ken Boyer, Bill White, Dick Groat and Ray Sadecki. Those deals helped the Cardinals win the National League pennant in 1967 and 1968. By that time, Howsam was in Cincinnati, laying the foundation for Reds teams that won the NL crown in 1970, 1972, 1975 and 1976 and the World Series in 1975 and 1976.

Cardinals

24
January

Happy Birthday, Cliff Heathcote— born on this date in 1898. The Cardinals traded him to the Cubs for Max Flack in between games of a separate-admission Memorial Day doubleheader in Chicago on May 30, 1922, which allowed both players to play for two teams in one day. In the morning game, Heathcote was 0-for-three as a Cardinal while Flack was hitless in four at-bats for the Cubs. The Cubs won 4-1. The two players traded uniforms before the second tilt in the afternoon. Heathcote collected two hits in four at-bats for Chicago while Flack was one-for-three for St. Louis. The Cubs won again, this time 3-1. Flack and Heathcote had remarkably similar careers. Flack played in 1,411 career games and Heathcote in 1,415. Flack hit .278 and Heathcote .275. Flack stole 200 bases, and Heathcote swiped 190. Flack had 212 doubles, and Heathcote garnered 206. Heathcote outhomered Flack 42-35. The only other player besides Flack and Heathcote to play for two teams in one day was Joel Youngblood with the Mets and Expos on August 4, 1982. Youngblood went one better, however, playing in two cities. He played for the Mets in Chicago in the afternoon, and after hopping a plane, appeared in the Expos-Phillies clash in Philadelphia that evening.

Cardinals

25
January

The question of the day: What was the Gas House Gang?

Although the 1934 world champion Cardinals (featuring a rowdy crew that included Dizzy Dean, Joe Medwick, Pepper Martin, Frankie Frisch and Leo Durocher) has gone into history as the "Gas House Gang," the name wasn't firmly established until late in the 1935 season. The origins of the name are somewhat murky. The most probable explanation derived from a double-header the Cards played in Boston in June 1935. It rained during the second game, leaving their uniforms caked with dirt. The team had to grab a late train for New York for a game against the Giants and there was no time to dry-clean the jerseys. They were still mud-stained when they took the field at the Polo Grounds. A reporter in the press box commented that the Cardinals looked like they were from the Gas House district, an area on the Lower East Side of Manhattan that housed a large number of gas tanks. It was a rough neighborhood and the subject of many novels and newspaper stories. The neighborhood included a vicious band of thugs known as the Gas House Gang, which flourished from about 1890 through 1910.

Cardinals

26
January

The question of the day: What was the legacy of the Gas House Gang?

Influential New York writers and cartoonists began referring to the Cardinals as the Gas House Gang because of the club's unkempt appearance and its willingness to do anything possible to win, including fisticuffs, and the nickname stuck. After winning the World Series in 1934, however, the Gas House Gang didn't reach the postseason again. The Cardinals had much more success, in fact, in the years immediately before and after the Gas House Gang. The Cards won the NL pennant in 1926, 1928, 1930 and 1931. The only individuals to play at least 100 games or pitch at least 100 innings for both the 1931 and 1934 pennant-winners were second baseman Frankie Frisch (who also managed the 1934 club), outfielder-third baseman Pepper Martin and pitcher Wild Bill Hallahan. Finishes of sixth place in 1932 and fifth in 1933 led to an almost complete transformation of the roster. By 1941, there were no more members of the 1934 team left with the Cardinals. The club won pennants again in 1942, 1943, 1944 and 1946.

Cardinals

27
January

In anticipation of the closing of the original Busch Stadium at Grand and Dozier, the Cardinals donated the land it occupied to the Herbert Hoover Boys Club (today known as the Herbert Hoover Boys and Girls Club) on this date in 1966. The ballpark closed the following May, and the Cards began playing downtown at the second Busch Stadium. The site had been used for baseball for 100 years, with the first amateur games there in 1866. The Cardinals played at Grand and Dozier from 1882 through 1892 and again from 1920 through 1966. It was converted into a complex serving 2,500 youngsters, including a recreation center and swimming pool. August Busch said he considered turning the park over to real estate interests for a shopping development but decided granting the land to the youth of St. Louis "would be beneficial to the entire community."

Cardinals

28
January

On this date in 1953, Cardinals owner Fred Saigh was convicted in federal court for income tax evasion. The judge sentenced him to 15 months in prison and imposed a $15,000 fine. The government charged that Saigh owed $558,901 in back taxes and penalties. He professed his innocence and declared that the sentence was too harsh, but under pressure from National League president Ford Frick, he decided to sell the Cardinals. The franchise was purchased by the Anheuser-Busch Brewery on February 20 for $3.75 million. Saigh said he could have made another $700,000 to $750,000 by selling the club to a group that intended to move the Cardinals out of town. He did make money investing in Anheuser-Busch, though. Saigh realized that the brewery's ownership of the Cardinals would benefit the company, and just before selling the club, he purchased 28,000 shares of stock in Anheuser-Busch. The day after the sale, the stock rose two dollars a share. For years, Saigh owned more stock in the brewery than anyone outside of the Busch family. The stock made him millions as Anheuser-Busch jumped from third in the market, behind Schlitz and Miller, to number one. When he died in 1999 at the age of 94, Saigh's net worth was estimated at $500 million.

Cardinals

29
January

Today's trivia: Which Cardinals player caught rabbit fever?

Playing in his second season in the majors, Enos Slaughter batted .320 with 12 homers and a league-leading 52 doubles in 1939. To reach those figures, Slaughter had to overcome an illness commonly known as rabbit fever, along with personal tragedy.

On New Year's morning, Enos and his father had gone rabbit hunting near their home in North Carolina. As they waded through underbrush, they were scratched by sharp thorns, and then they shot and handled infected rabbits. That afternoon, Slaughter's father became ill and was bedridden. Eleven days later he died of "rabbit fever," called tularemia. Enos also contracted the ailment and hovered for weeks between life and death. Rabbit fever strikes its victims with a high temperature that comes and goes. Weakness, depression, and abscesses develop. Still suffering, Slaughter reported to spring training against the wishes of his doctor and family. He shivered under the hot Florida sun, and the abscesses caused great pain with almost every move, but he kept the illness from Cardinals management for fear of losing his place in the starting line-up. He went on to have a terrific season.

Cardinals

30
January

The question of the day: What Cardinals pitcher changed his uniform number to correspond with the number of wins he was seeking?

Mort Cooper, who normally wore number 13, had been trying to win his 14th game for more than a month in 1942. To change his luck, Cooper donned Gus Mancuso's number 14 for a game against the Reds on August 14 and won 4-0 on a two-hitter. For the rest of the season, Cooper wore a uniform number that corresponded to the victory total he was seeking. He won seven games in seven consecutive starts, finishing the year by winning the National League Most Valuable Player Award with a 22-7 record, ten shutouts, and a 1.73 ERA. The earned run average was the lowest of any NL pitcher between 1920 and 1967.

31
January

Happy Birthday, Tom Alston, who was born on this date in 1926. His full name was Thomas Edison Alston. He became the Cardinals' first African-American player by making his major league debut on April 13, 1954. He was hitless in four at-bats of a 13-4 win over the Cubs at Busch Stadium. The Cardinals purchased Alston from San Diego in the Pacific Coast league for $100,000. A first baseman who stood six-foot-five, Alston was viewed as a can't-miss prospect and appeared to be a star when he homered in his second and third major league games. But he hit only .244 with four homers in 271 at-bats over four seasons in the majors. The Cardinals were the 10th of the then 16 teams in the majors to integrate. The club continued to add minority players throughout the remainder of the 1950s, and by 1959, there were seven African-Americans on the roster including Bob Gibson, Bill White and Curt Flood. The only club with more black or Latin players in 1959 was the San Francisco Giants with nine.

Cardinals

February

Cardinals

01
February

The question of the day: When did the Cardinals order satin uniforms?

The Cardinals purchased red satin uniforms in 1946 for night games on the road instead of the traditional gray outfits. When the uniforms arrived, however, the club considered them to be too gaudy. The suits were donated to the North Side Teen Town team of the St. Louis Muny League. Several clubs tried the satin material during the 1940s. Baseball officials believed the reflective material would add to the enjoyment of the sport under the lights, but the outfits were almost impossible to keep clean and were uncomfortable on hot and humid summer evenings.

Cardinals

02
February

On this date in 1961, a spokesman for the Vinoy Park Hotel in St. Petersburg, Florida, which served as the Cardinals' spring training head-quarters, informed the club that African-American players would have to find quarters elsewhere. C. H. Alberding of Tulsa, Oklahoma, the president of the company that operated the hotel, said that if the Cardinals insisted on housing all of their personnel in the same hotel, the team should "look for other hotels." The statement came after the Cardinals requested that the entire club stay in one hotel. Bing Devine, the Cards' general manager, said segregation caused problems, but added, "We don't make the rules and regulations for various localities." Since the Cardinals had integrated the roster in 1954, African-American players lived and ate at private homes and rooming houses during spring training. It was a problem throughout spring training as clubs trained in towns and cities in Florida where segregation had been entrenched by both law and custom for decades. St. Petersburg was among those cities. The Vinoy Park Hotel opened in 1925. It closed in 1974 and was a haven for vagrants until a $93 million renovation during the 1990s restored it to one of the top hotels in St. Petersburg.

Cardinals

03
February

The question of the day: How did the Cardinals resolve the issue of segregated housing during spring training?

The walls of segregation in the South were just beginning to crack during the early 1960s, led by Civil Rights groups such as the Southern Christian Leadership Conference and the Freedom Riders, which were in the news on an almost daily basis. Under prodding from African-American players with the Cardinals, led by Bill White, Curt Flood and Bob Gibson, the situation changed in 1962 when August Busch leased two adjoining hotels near the Skyway Bridge that allowed the club's black and white players to stay together. The Yankees left St. Petersburg after the 1961 season and moved to Fort Lauderdale in 1962, in part due to the racial restrictions in the Tampa Bay area. The Yanks had trained in St. Pete since 1925. The Mets subsequently used St. Petersburg as a training site from 1962 through 1987. The Cards were in St. Pete from 1938 through 1997, with the exception of three seasons (1943–45) during World War II.

Cardinals

04
February

The question of the day: How was the construction of the second Busch Stadium financed?

August Busch was used to getting his own way. He wanted a new stadium for the Cardinals in downtown St. Louis that could comfortably hold 50,000 fans and demanded that the stockholders of Anheuser-Busch, Inc., approve a $5 million investment for the construction of the facility. The motion passed by a 7-1 margin on April 13, 1960. The other $21 million necessary to make the stadium a reality was raised by the Civic Center Development Corporation, headed by James P. Hickok, president of the First National Bank of St. Louis; Sidney Maestra, chairman of the Mercantile Trust, Co.; and Preston Estep, president of the Transit Casualty, Co. The Civic Center Development Corporation would become the owners of the new ballpark, which opened on May 13, 1966, with the unwieldy name Civic Center Busch Memorial Stadium. (By 1983, it was known simply as Busch Stadium.) It was one of only three privately financed stadium built for Major League Baseball since 1923. The other two are Dodger Stadium in Los Angeles in 1962 and AT&T Park in San Francisco in 2000.

Cardinals

05
February

Happy Birthday, Chuck Diering, who was born on this date in 1923 in St. Louis, Missouri. In 1941, after an excellent high school career, he was signed by the Cardinals. He played with Albany of the Georgia-Florida League in 1942 and batted .305 in 126 games. On February 4, 1943, Diering began serving in the U.S. Army both in the United States and the Pacific. He was a private first-class and worked at the orthopedic clinic of the 44th General Hospital at Fort Sill. He made his major league debut for the Cardinals in 1947 as a back-up centerfielder who appeared in 105 games with only 74 at-bats. In 1949, he became the regular centerfielder and appeared in 131 games with a .263 batting average. As a local product, he was a fan favorite. Though he was never much of a hitter, Diering possessed great speed and was an outstanding fielder. He was traded to the New York Giants in 1951, where he dazzled fans with his glove. In 1954, after a year in the minors, he was drafted by the new Baltimore Orioles and was selected the team MVP for his amazing defensive plays. After his career ended, he settled in St. Louis, where he continues to be a popular local "boy," even as he nears 90 years of age.

Cardinals

06
February

Happy Birthday, Bill Dawley. William Chester Dawley was born on this date in 1958 in Norwich, Connecticut. Big Bill—he was 6'5" and 240 pounds—was selected in the seventh round of the 1976 draft by the Reds but was traded to the Astros organization, where he made his major league debut in 1983. Since he was not an early-round pick and was deemed suited only for middle relief, expectations were low, but Dawley surprised everyone by pitching well enough to be selected to the NL All-Star team in his rookie year. The following season he was even better, posting an 11-4 record and 1.93 ERA, all in relief. But hitters seemed to figure him out the next year, and following a trade to the White Sox, Dawley joined the Cardinals in 1987 for the pennant-winning season, posting a 5-8 record with 65 strikeouts and a 4.47 ERA, though he was not included on the post-season roster. St. Louis released him at the end of the year and his career ended two years later. The seventh round of the '76 draft turned out to be a great one for the Cards as Willie McGee and Ozzie Smith were also both selected—McGee by the White Sox and Smith by Detroit. Neither signed that year.

Cardinals

07
February

Happy Birthday, Benny Ayala. Don't remember him as a Cardinal? Well, you can be forgiven for the lapse in memory since he played all of one game for the Redbirds. (February 7 was a slow day in Cardinal history.) Benigno Ayala Felix was born on this date in 1951 in Yauco, Puerto Rico, and made his major league debut with the New York Mets in 1974, hitting a home run in his first at-bat. But he didn't hit many more and was traded in 1977 to the Cards, who hoped he would produce the power he'd shown in the minors. He was sent to Triple-A New Orleans, where, in fact, he hit 18 homers and 27 doubles to post a .500 slugging percentage. And he did compile a .333 batting average for the Cardinals—one hit in three at-bats. He was sent back to the minors in 1978 and struggled at the plate. The Cardinals traded him in January 1979 to the Orioles, where he was used primarily as a designated hitter. But even though he only sipped a cup of coffee in St. Louis, we raise a glass to him on his birthday.

Cardinals

08
February

Happy Birthday, Keith McDonald, who was born on this date in 1973 in Yokosuka, Japan. McDonald made his major league debut on July 4, 2000, and hit a home run in his first at-bat as a pinch-hitter in the eighth inning of a 14-3 win over the Reds at Busch Stadium. Two days later, he became only the second batter to homer in his first two at-bats in the majors. Placed in the line-up as a catcher, McDonald homered in the second inning of a 12-6 triumph over the Reds in St. Louis. The only other player to homer in his first two at-bats in the majors was Bob Nieman of the St. Louis Browns on September 14, 1951. McDonald had one of the most peculiar careers in big league history. He was 27 when he reached the majors. Despite his fast start, McDonald played in only eight major league games and accumulated only nine at-bats over two seasons (2000–01). After hitting homers in his first two at-bats, McDonald collected only one more hit in the majors, which was also a home run in his sixth career at-bat. His final big league batting record included three hits, three homers, a .333 batting average, a .455 on-base percentage, and a 1.333 slugging percentage. McDonald is also the only player with more than one home run but no other hits.

Cardinals

09
February

Happy Birthday, Specs Toporcer, who was born on this date in 1899. Toporcer was an infielder with the Cardinals from 1921 through 1928. A 9-5 win over the Cubs on June 23, 1923, at Sportsman's Park was enlivened by an argument on the field between Toporcer, playing shortstop, and St. Louis pitcher Fred Toney. In the fourth inning, Toney wanted Toporcer to move closer to third base when Cliff Heathcote came to bat. Toporcer refused to budge, and Heathcote drove a ball through the spot where Toney had suggested Toporcer position himself. Toney blew up at Toporcer in full view of the fans. Specs took off his glasses and raised his fists before Toney returned to the mound. In the bottom of the inning, Toporcer was cheered when he came to bat and Toney was booed. Toney refused to take his place in the batter's box and stormed off the field. The pitcher said he was quitting baseball, but Branch Rickey, who at the time was serving as both field manager and general manager, was critical of Toporcer for refusing to move and convinced Toney to return to the club two days later. In his next start five days later, Toney pitched a shutout to beat Grover Alexander and the Cubs 1-0 in Chicago.

Cardinals

10
February

Happy Birthday, Curt Welch, who was born on this date in 1862. Welch was an outfielder with the Cardinals from 1885 through 1887. On June 18, 1887, he was arrested during a game against the Orioles in Baltimore that resulted in an 8-8 tie. In the ninth inning, Welch tried to steal second base but ran outside the base line and slammed hard into second baseman Bill Greenwood, causing Greenwood to drop the ball and turn a complete somersault. As Baltimore players ran onto the field to check on Greenwood's condition, they found he had severely injured his back. A number of spectators ran onto the field and rushed toward Welch. Police sprang into action to head off the mob, and surrounded the St. Louis players. Welch was arrested for assault on Greenwood, and the Cardinal outfielder was marched to the clubhouse. Fearing a riot, umpire Jack McQuaid ended the contest and declared it a draw. Welch was taken to jail, where he was released on $200 bail. The following day, Welch stood trial and was fined $4.50.

Cardinals

11
February

The question of the day: What was Whitey Ball?

The Cardinals of the 1980s were one of the most unusual teams in baseball history. The club won three NL pennants in 1982, 1985 and 1987 with the lowest home runs totals in baseball at the time, and the highest stolen base figures since the pre-1920 Dead Ball Era. With Whitey Herzog directing the club from the bench, the style of play became known as "Whitey Ball." Hired to run the Cardinals in June 1980, Herzog tailored his club around the dimensions and surface of the second Busch Stadium, with distant fences and Astroturf, by acquiring players with blazing speed. During a ten-year span from 1982 through 1991, the Cardinals ranked last in the majors in home runs nine times. The exception was 1985, when the Cards were 25th among 26 teams. Over the same period, the club was first in the NL in stolen bases seven times (consecutively from 1982 through 1988), were second three times, and first in the majors five seasons (five in a row from 1984 through 1988). The peak year was 1985, when the Cards stole 314 bases, which is still the most of any major league team since the 1912 New York Giants swiped 319.

Cardinals

12 February

The question of the day: Where did Cards owner Sam Breadon want to build a stadium?

During the 1947 season, Breadon placed a sign at the northwest corner of Spring and Choteau on property he had owned since 1924. The sign read: "New stadium for the Cardinals to be erected on this 14 acres." The 14 acres were bounded by Choteau, Spring, Gratiot and Grand Boulevard. The stadium was never erected, however. In the 1940s, government tax money was seldom used to build stadiums. Clubs had to bear 100 percent of the construction costs, and post-war inflation pushed the stadium project beyond what Breadon was willing to pay. He was also past his 70th birthday, and his health was failing. Breadon sold the Cardinals the following November.

Cardinals

13
February

Happy Birthday, Dick Hughes, who was born on this date in 1938. He struck out 13 batters for the Cardinals on May 30, 1967, but lost a heartbreaking 2-1 decision to the Reds at Crosley Field. Hughes retired the first 21 batters he faced before the Reds scored twice in the eighth on Tony Perez's triple, Vada Pinson's double and a single by Leo Cardenas. In the Cardinal ninth, Orlando Cepeda and Tim McCarver opened with singles, and Cincinnati manager Dave Bristol replaced Jim Maloney with Don Nottebart. On Nottebart's first pitch, Phil Gagliano hit a grounder to shortstop Cardenas, who flipped to Tommy Helms at second to start what appeared to be a double play. Helms threw to Deron Johnson at first for the second out. But Cepeda, running hard all the way from second base, headed home in an attempt to score the tying run. Johnson alertly fired the ball to catcher Johnny Edwards, who tagged out Cepeda for a game-ending 6-4-3-2 triple play. Hughes had a record of 16-6 with a 2.67 ERA as a 29-year-old rookie in 1967. With thick glasses, the result of 20-300 vision in one eye, he didn't look like an athlete. Hughes developed arm trouble and recorded only two wins after his stellar 1967 season.

Cardinals

14
February

The Cardinals signed John Mabry as a free agent on this date in 2004. On May 2, 2005, Mabry capped the greatest ninth-inning comeback in club history to beat the Reds 10-9 at Great American Ballpark. With the Cards down 9-3 in the top of the inning, Reds reliever David Weathers walked Yadier Molina and Abraham Nunez. After Roger Cedeno struck out, David Eckstein singled to load the bases. Albert Pujols hit into a force out, scoring Molina. At this point, the Cardinals were one out away from losing and trailed by five runs. Reggie Sanders kept the rally alive by singling in Nunez, and Danny Graves replaced Weathers. Jim Edmonds got the Reds fans murmuring with a three-run homer off Graves to make it 9-8. Mark Grudzielanek reached first base on an error by first baseman Sean Casey, and Mabry followed with a homer to put the Cardinals into the lead and ultimately won the game.

Cardinals

15
February

Happy Birthday, Cub Stricker, who was born on this date in 1860. He was the second of five managers employed by eccentric owner Chris Von Der Ahe in 1892. Jack Glassock started the season as manager. One of the best shortstops in baseball during the 1880s, Glassock was 34 years old in 1892 and past his peak, but was still an effective player. Unfortunately, he couldn't stomach Von Der Ahe's interference and lasted only four games as skipper, although he remained the starting shortstop. Cub Stricker, a feisty infielder, followed Glassock and compiled a 6-17 record as manager before Von Der Ahe dismissed him. Two weeks prior to being fired, Stricker jumped into the Sportsman's Park seats following a 10-2 loss and punched a fan who had been heckling the team. Jack Crooks was the third manager and had a record of 27-33. George Gore, a star outfielder with Chicago during the 1880s, became the next man to guide the Cardinals. Gore was 35 and near the end of his career. He was 6-9 as manager and batted .205 in 20 games. Bob Caruthers, another 1880s star in the last throes of his playing career, finished out the season and was 16-32 as manager.

Cardinals

16
February

The question of the day: Why did the Cardinals hold spring training in St. Louis in 1919?

The Cardinals held spring training drills in St. Louis in 1919 because the club didn't have the cash to head south. Manager Branch Rickey had the club work out at Washington University. Stockholder A. M. Diaz, who had made money selling shoemakers' tools and supplies, agreed to house the players and buy equipment for the training camp. The coaches guarded the baseballs so the team wouldn't have to foot the bill for new ones. The uniforms from the year before that were salvageable were sent to seamstresses for patching, and others were borrowed from semipro and high school teams. Rickey found a sporting goods store that would make the rest of the jerseys and extend him credit. With the exception of World War II, when travel was restricted, the 1919 Cardinals and Philadelphia Athletics were the last two clubs to conduct spring training in their home city.

Cardinals

17
February

The question of the day: What two bizarre events took place during a 17-4 loss to the Diamondbacks in Phoenix on April 17, 2001?

During the game, pitcher Gene Stechschulte, acting as a pinch-hitter, homered in his first major league at-bat, and first baseman Bobby Bonilla, acting as a pitcher, gave up a home run to the first batter he faced. Stechschulte, who had played in 25 previous games as a reliever but never batted, was sent to the plate as a pinch-hitter in the sixth inning and hit a home run off Armando Reynoso. Not only did Stechschulte homer in his first at-bat, but on the first pitch as well. Bonilla, appearing in the last season of his 16-year career, took the mound in the ninth for the first time ever. Erubiel Durazo, the first batter he faced, hit a home run. Bonilla allowed two runs in the inning. Stechschulte collected just five at-bats in his career and had two hits for a .400 batting average. The other base hit was a single in his second at-bat.

Cardinals

18
February

The question of the day: When and where did the first Sunday game in National League history take place?

The National League was founded in 1876, but didn't allow its teams to play on Sunday until 1892. The first Sunday game took place on April 17 with the Cardinals losing 5-1 to the Reds at Sportsman's Park in St. Louis. Because of local laws, however, the only two teams permitted to play on Sunday in 1892 were the Cardinals and the Reds. Chicago was cleared to play on the Christian Sabbath in 1893, but it would be well into the 20th century before the other NL teams could play at home on Sunday because state or local laws banned the practice. The New York Giants and Brooklyn Dodgers were allowed to do so for the first time in 1919, the Boston Braves in 1929, and the Pirates and Phillies in 1934.

Cardinals

19
February

Today's trivia: Who was the most versatile player in Cards history? You could make a great case for Jose Oquendo, who played for the Redbirds from 1986 to 1995 and spent time at all nine positions. On May 14, 1988, he was the losing pitcher when the Cardinals fell 7-5 in a 19-inning marathon to the Braves at Busch Stadium. Oquendo entered the game in the ninth as a first baseman. After pitching the 15th, Cardinals reliever Randy O'Neal developed a sore shoulder. He was the seventh St. Louis pitcher in the game. The only three hurlers left were starters and weren't available. Whitey Herzog had also used all of his position players. And so he sent Oquendo to the mound. Jose DeLeon, who had pitched 8⅔ innings the night before, went to the outfield. He played right field against right-handed batters and left field against left-handers, switching back and forth with Tom Brunansky. Amazingly, Oquendo shutout the Braves in the 16th, 17th and 18th innings. In the 19th, Ken Griffey, Sr. hit a two-out, two-run double to give Atlanta the victory. During his career, Oquendo appeared in 649 games at second base, 364 at shortstop, 58 at third base, 47 in right field, 23 at first base, 11 in left field, seven in center, three as a pitcher and one as a catcher.

Cardinals

20 February

On this date in 1953, the Anheuser-Busch brewery purchased the Cardinals for $3.75 million from Fred Saigh. August Busch became president of the club. Saigh was forced to sell because of a conviction for income tax evasion. He received lucrative bids from groups in Houston that intended to move the Cardinals to Texas. Saigh also entertained offers from interests in Milwaukee, which had just completed County Stadium, opened in 1952, with the idea of luring a big-league club. Saigh said he wanted to keep the team in St. Louis, however. Busch was 53 years old when his brewery purchased the Cardinals. He had become president of the company in 1946. His great-grandfather, Adolphus Busch, founded the brewery with Eberhard Anheuser in 1865. Before he bought the Cards, Busch was better known in St. Louis social circles for hobbies such as horsemanship and hunting and for his lavish parties. He was a casual baseball fan, but he had the idea that buying the Cardinals would be good for the brewery's relationship with the city and would boost sales. Over time, Busch became a major power broker in baseball circles. He died in 1989 at the age of 90. The Busch family continued to own the Cardinals until 1996.

Cardinals

21
February

Wilmer "Vinegar Bend" Mizell died on this date in 1999. He pitched for the Cardinals in 1952 and 1953 and again from 1956 thorough 1960. Mizell earned the nickname because he hailed from the small Alabama town of Vinegar Bend, although he was born in Leakesville, Mississippi, just across the state line. With his appealing Southern drawl, many billed him as the next Dizzy Dean. Mizell never came close to emulating Dean's Hall of Fame career, but he was an effective middle-of-the-rotation starter and compiled a record of 69-70 as a Cardinal. After his playing days ended, Mizell went into politics. He was elected to the US Congress in 1968 as a Republican from North Carolina and served until losing a reelection bid in 1974. Later, Mizell served as an Assistant Secretary of Commerce under Ronald Reagan, and as an executive director of the President's Council on Physical Fitness under the elder George Bush.

Cardinals

22
February

The question of the day: What future member of the College and Pro Football Hall of Fame played minor league baseball with the Cardinals?

Sammy Baugh was the number one overall pick in the 1937 National Football League draft. After establishing himself as one of the best quarterbacks in football while playing for the Washington Redskins during his rookie season, Baugh decided to give baseball a try. He had been a star in both baseball and football while at Texas Christian University. He played in 53 games as a shortstop for the Cardinals' minor league clubs in Columbus and Rochester in 1938, but he hit only .200. He returned to football and had a career that lasted until 1951. Baugh was in the first class of 16 inductees in the pro Football Hall of Fame in 1963.

Cardinals

23
February

On this date in 1943, the Cardinals advertised for players in *The Sporting News*. With the military and enlistments taking players out of the organization, both at the major and minor league levels, the Cardinals took an unusual step in securing replacements for the club in the farm system. "If you are now a free agent and have previous professional experience, we may be able to place you to your advantage on one of our clubs," the ad read. "We have positions open on our AA, B and D classification clubs." The ad asked players to submit their previous professional experience, playing position, marital status, date of birth, height, weight, and Selective Service classification.

Cardinals

24 February

The question of the day: Where did the Cardinals conduct spring training during World War II?

During World War II, teams had to train north of the Ohio River and east of the Mississippi to save on travel expenses. The Cards trained at Cairo, Illinois, a town at the confluence of the Ohio and Mississippi, prior to the 1943, 1944 and 1945 seasons before returning to St. Petersburg, Florida, in 1946. When the Midwest spring weather prevented outdoor practice, the Cardinals trained at a high school gymnasium in Cairo. The 1946 major league training camps were unique as returning war veterans competed with wartime fill-ins for spots on the roster. The Cardinals' spring training roster included 22 players who had spent all or most of the 1945 season in the military.

Cardinals

25
February

On this date in 1972, the Cardinals traded Steve Carlton to the Phillies for Rick Wise. Carlton and August Busch were involved in a bitter contract dispute during the 1969–70 off-season, and Carlton signed a two-year deal worth $45,000 a season. After compiling a 20-9 record in 1971, Carlton wanted a large raise. At the same time, as an inflation-checking device, President Richard Nixon ordered wage and price controls with annual salary increases fixed at no more than 5.5 percent. Busch was determined to follow Nixon's directives, even though professional athletes were exempt from the salary controls. Carlton believed his 20-win season should be enough to increase his salary to the $65,000 range. The negotiations were complicated by Busch's personal dislike of the pitcher. During a time when the generation gap was a chasm, the 72-year-old Busch didn't understand the 27-year-old Carlton's fascination with martial arts and Eastern religions. The possibility of a player's strike, which would eventually wipe out the first week of the regular season, also put Busch in a disagreeable mood. In the end, Busch ordered general manager Bing Devine to trade Carlton, who was swapped for Rick Wise of the Phillies. Wise was locked in a contract dispute of his own. Ironically, Busch paid Wise the same salary that Carlton was seeking.

Cardinals

26
February

The question of the day: What was the result of the Carlton-Wise trade?

When the trade was completed, it looked to be about even. Over the previous two seasons, Carlton had an ERA of 3.64. Wise's ERA over the same period was 3.45. Wise was also nine months younger than Carlton. As things turned out, the Cards got the lesser of the exchange. In 1972, Carlton was 27-10 with a Philadelphia club that went 59-97. After leaving the Cardinals, he won 252 big league games to finish his career 329-244. He seemed to save his best for Cardinals match-ups, compiling a 38-14 mark against his former club. In two seasons with the Redbirds, before a trade to the Red Sox, Wise posted a 32-28 record and had a 3.24 ERA, but he pitched without much support from hitters and relievers. He went to Boston with Bernie Carbo on October 26, 1973, for Reggie Smith and Ken Tatum.

Cardinals

27
February

Today's trivia: Which Cards pitcher produced one of the greatest seasons in team history in 1934? Dizzy Dean posted a 30-7 record and a 2.66 ERA in 311⅔ innings over 50 games, 33 of them starts, in 1934. He was 26-5 as a starter with 24 complete games. In his 17 relief assignments, he was 4-2 with seven saves and a 2.90 ERA in 31 innings. From August 4 through the end of the regular season, Dean pitched 106⅓ innings over a period of 58 days in 11 starts and eight relief appearances. He was 11-3 with an ERA of 1.35. Win number 30 came on the final day of the regular season. With the Giants only one game behind, the Cards needed a victory against the Reds in St. Louis. Pitching on only one day of rest, Dean won 9-0. It was his second complete game shutout in three days. Three days later, he started game one of the World Series, and defeated the Tigers 8-3 with another complete game. Counting the Fall Classic, Dean hurled 132⅓ innings in 67 days and had a 13-4 record with an earned run average of 1.43.

Cardinals

28
February

Today's trivia: When did the Cardinals play a 27-inning doubleheader without scoring a run?

The Cardinals played 27 innings on July 2, 1933, and suffered a pair of crushing 1-0 losses against the Giants at the Polo Grounds. The Cards collected only ten hits in the twinbill. The first game lasted 18 innings. In a remarkable performance, future Hall of Famer Carl Hubbell hurled a complete game shutout for New York, allowing only six hits and no walks. St. Louis wasted the pitching excellence of Tex Carleton, who tossed the first 16 innings for the Cards before being lifted for a pinch-hitter. Jesse Haines pitched the 17th and 18th innings. The game ended on a single by Hughie Critz. It is the fifth-longest 1-0 game in major league history. In the second contest, Dizzy Dean lost a 1-0 duel to Roy Parmelee. A homer by Johnny Vergez in the fourth inning provided the lone run of the game. The first game lasted four hours and three minutes and the second just one hour and 25 minutes.

Cardinals

29
February

Happy Birthday, Pepper Martin, who was born on this date in 1904. When the 1931 World Series began, Martin was an unheralded 27-year-old rookie outfielder with the Cardinals who hit .300 with seven homers during the regular season. By the end of the Series, Martin was a national hero for his play in a seven-game defeat of the Philadelphia Athletics. After the first five games, Martin had 12 hits in 18 at-bats. Among his hits were four doubles and a home run. He also stole four bases, scored five runs, and drove in five. Although he would add his fifth stolen base of the Series, Martin went hitless in six at-bats over the final two games. But his teammates picked up the slack, and the Cardinals managed to win the World Series. There was also an unusual incident prior to game six. During fielding practice, a man with a rifle rushed toward Martin. It turned out to be a gun manufacturer, who presented the rifle to Martin, an avid hunter, as a gift. Martin was a stocky five-foot-eight and hailed from rural Oklahoma. Making up for limited talent, he won over fans with his desperate, reckless, all-out hustle that earned him the nickname "The Wild Horse of the Osage." Martin played his last game for the Cardinals in 1944.

Cardinals

March

Cardinals

01
March

Happy Birthday, Harry Caray, who was born on this date in 1915 and christened Harry Christopher Carabina. He began broadcasting major league baseball in 1945. At the time, two stations with two sets of announcers carried the Cardinals and Browns home games. As a matter of policy that had been in effect for more than a decade, single games on Sunday and the first games of Sunday and holiday doubleheaders were blacked out, as were both teams' road games. France Laux and Johnny O'Hara were on WTMV. Caray and Gabby Street were behind the mic on WIL. Caray replaced Dizzy Dean in 1945. Dean, whose playing career ended in 1941, left the broadcasting booth for a year as a "goodwill ambassador" for Falstaff Beer—touring Army bases and hospitals, showing baseball films and telling yarns about the Gas House Gang. He also pitched a few exhibition games against Negro Leagues star Satchel Paige. In 1946, Caray was named the number one announcer in the National League by *The Sporting News.* That same year, Dean returned to broadcast Cardinals and Browns games, replacing France Laux. Caray remained the Cardinals' play-by-play voice until 1969.

Cardinals

02
March

Today's trivia: When did Cardinals games move to television?

All of the Cardinals and Browns home games were on television in 1947. Harry Caray and Gabby Street announced the Cardinals games while the Browns had Dizzy Dean and Johnny O'Hara. There was also a change to the radio broadcasts. Prior to 1947, the teams agreed to broadcast only home games for fear that airing road games while the other was playing at home would harm attendance. Beginning in 1947, the Cardinals broke the blackout agreement, and stations broadcast road games for the first time. Cards owner Sam Breadon also created controversy by choosing Caray and Street as his team over Dean and O'Hara. At the time, Caray had only done play-by-play for two years, and many didn't like his bombastic style. Dean, on the other hand, was a St. Louis institution. Caray and Gabby Street were also on WEW in St. Louis and WTMV in East St. Louis, two stations with less powerful signals than WIL, where Dean and O'Hara worked. When the teams began broadcasting road games in 1947, the announcers remained in St. Louis and re-created the games using updates from a Western Union ticker. As each play came in on the ticker, in code, a Western Union operator interpreted the message for the announcers, who then reconstructed the scene as if they were actually there. Announcers began traveling regularly with the club during the 1950s.

Cardinals

03
March

On this date in 1953, Lou Perini, owner of the Boston Braves, blocked an attempt by Browns' owner Bill Veeck to move his team from St. Louis to Milwaukee. Perini hoped to move his own team to the Wisconsin city that had recently built a new stadium in hopes of wooing a major league team. Though attendance at Browns games had improved in the past year, Veeck felt he had little chance of competing with August Busch, who had bought the Cardinals a few weeks earlier, on February 20. Veeck then tried to move the team to Baltimore, which also had just built a stadium and wanted a team of its own. But the American League blocked him, stating that it was too close to the start of the season. Veeck was stuck in St. Louis, trying in vain to draw fans who resented his attempts to move the team. Attendance plummeted and Veeck had to sell the team, which, in fact, moved to Baltimore the following year.

Cardinals

04
March

On this date in 2008, the Cardinals signed starting pitcher Adam Wainwright to a four-year contract for $21 million. Since then he has compiled a 50-22 record and become one of the best pitchers in the National League, but he earlier had made MLB history with his bat rather than his arm. On May 24, 2006, he went to the plate for the first at-bat of his career and hit a home run off Noah Lowry of the Giants. In fact, he went yard with the first pitch of his first major league at-bat, becoming only the 22nd batter in MLB history to accomplish the feat, the 11th National Leaguer. In 337 plate appearances during his career, Wainwright has hit a total of five homers.

05
March

On this date in 1917, Helene Britton sold the Cardinals to a group of St. Louis investors headed by James C. Jones. Jones was Helene's business advisor and briefly served as team president in 1912. Jones was worried that out-of-town interests would buy the Cardinals and pull the club out of the city. His idea was to make the Cardinals community-owned. He paid $375,000 for the club by lining up 1,200 investors who bought stock in $25 shares with $10,000 as the maximum amount. As an incentive to purchase the stock, Jones came up with a clever idea. Anyone who bought a share of stock had the right to give a season pass to a deserving underprivileged youngster between the ages of 10 and 16. Large organizations serving St. Louis youth were contacted to help identify those in need. Called the Knothole Gang, the program was credited with helping to curb juvenile delinquency. The free tickets also helped turn many St. Louis youngsters away from the Browns and made them lifelong Redbird fans. The plan to turn the Cardinals into a community-owned organization was unworkable, however. The franchise was on the verge of bankruptcy when his group bought the club in 1917, and the situation didn't improve under his leadership. Sam Breadon bought the franchise in 1920 and owned it until 1947.

On this date in 1923, the Cardinals announced that they would use uniforms numbers for the upcoming season. At the time, no club in the majors placed numbers on uniforms, although they had been in use by college football teams for years. Previously, baseball clubs had numbers for each player on the scorecards and posted the corresponding number on the scoreboard as each player came to bat to help the fans identify the players, and in some cases, the full batting order was placed on the scoreboards. The numbers on the 1923 Cardinals' uniforms were about six inches high on the left sleeve, but were so small that it was almost impossible to read them from the stands. The experiment was dropped before the season was over, in part because concessionaires complained about the drop in scorecard sales. The first club to use permanent numbers on the backs of uniforms was the Yankees in 1929. By 1932, all clubs in the majors affixed numbers to their uniforms.

07
March

The question of the day: Why did the Cardinals trade Keith Hernandez on June 15, 1983?

At the time, there seemed to be little explanation for the trade that sent Keith Hernandez to the Mets for pitchers Neil Allen and Rick Ownbey. It came out later, however, that Hernandez and Whitey Herzog had a strained relationship over Keith's involvement in drugs. Also, Herzog loved guys who scrapped and rolled around in the dirt, and Hernandez was never that kind of player. While with the Mets, Hernandez kicked his drug habit and was a regular for five more years, played in three more All-Star Games, and won another World Series ring to go with the one he earned as a Cardinal in 1982. The Cards received next to nothing in the deal. Allen was an average pitcher at best, while Ownbey compiled a 1-6 record in a St. Louis uniform.

Cardinals

08
March

Former President William Howard Taft died on this date in 1930. During his second year as president, Taft visited both St. Louis ballparks on May 4, 1910. A native of Cincinnati, Taft started the day by attending two innings of the Cardinals 12-3 win over the Reds at League Park at the corner of Vandeveter and Natural Bridge. The portly president, who weighed over 300 pounds, was provided with a comfortable armchair to watch the game. To avoid showing favoritism, Taft walked the three blocks to Sportsman's Park at Grand Avenue and Dodier Street to witness part of the Browns-Indians game, which ended in a 3-3 tie when it was called by darkness after 14 innings. By leaving early, Taft missed one of the strangest games in Cardinals history. The Cards scored their 12 runs on only four hits as three Cincinnati pitchers combined to walk 16 hitters. St. Louis plated seven runs in the third inning with only one base hit. Taft also witnessed the Cardinals defeat the Phillies 3-2 in St. Louis on September 23, 1911, and stayed all nine innings.

09
March

Today's trivia: How did the Cardinals come from behind to win the 1964 pennant race?

As late as August 23, the Cardinals were 11 games behind the first-place Phillies with 39 games remaining. On September 20, the Cardinals were tied for second place with Cincinnati and 6½ games back of Philadelphia with 13 contests left to play. But the Cards swept a five-game series against the Pirates in Pittsburgh from September 24 through September 27 while the Phillies lost seven in a row to the Reds and Milwaukee Braves. The Reds also swept the Mets in a five-game series in New York to take first place by one game over the Phillies and 1½ ahead of the Cards. The Phils came to Busch Stadium on September 28 for a three-game series and dropped all three to the Cardinals. At the end of the series, the Cardinals were in first place by one game over Cincinnati and 2½ over the Philadelphia. All that remained were three games in St. Louis against the Mets, a club with a 51-108 record. But the Mets stunned the Cards in the first two games of the series 1-0 and 15-5. The Cards needed a win on the final day to pull out a pennant, and did so with an 11-5 victory over New York to finish one game up on both the Reds and the Phillies.

Cardinals

10 March

The question of the day: How did Johnny Keane shock the Cardinals? Twice.

Keane guided the Cardinals to their tremendous comeback in 1964. In the World Series, he led them to a seven-game win over the Yankees, with the clincher coming in a 7-5 win on October 15. But the following day, Keane stunned the Cardinals by announcing his resignation. He had worked in the organization since 1938 and had been manager of the parent club since July 1961. The Cardinals called a press conference to announce Keane's new contract, but he showed up 15 minutes late and handed August Busch his resignation. After Busch fired general manager Bing Devine on August 17, Keane believed he would be the next to go and knew Busch was courting Leo Durocher. Busch had little choice but to retain Keane, however, after the world championship, but Keane had decided to leave. Three days after resigning, he shocked everyone again by becoming the manager of the Yankees. Yogi Berra had won the pennant in his first year as manager, but he was fired on October 16, the same day that Keane left the Cardinals. As soon as Keane took over, however, the Yankees dynasty ended. They finished sixth in 1965, the club's first losing season since 1925. After a 4-16 start in 1966, Keane was fired. On January 6, 1967, he died of a heart attack at the age of 55.

11
March

On this date in 1997, the Cardinals signed Bill Ortega as an amateur free agent. The Cuban native played in the organization for six years but managed only a brief September call-up to the majors in 2001. Unlike Moonlight Graham in the movie *Field of Dreams*, who played in an inning in right field but never got to bat, Ortega was called on as a pinch hitter five times but never got to play in the field in the majors. He did get a base hit in his five plate appearances, ending his MLB career with a .200 batting average. He struck out once. The following year he was sent back to AAA Memphis, where he hit .253 in 293 at-bats. He was then released by the team, ending his pro career without ever taking the field, though no doubt relishing his one major-league hit.

Cardinals

12 March

On this date in 1895, Cardinals owner Chris Von der Ahe assaulted an African-American man named George Stevenson. Defenseless and bewildered, Stevenson took a few punches to the face from Von der Ahe and then several shots at his feet. The attack was unprovoked, and Von der Ahe was arrested for felonious assault. He protested the charge, claiming that African-Americans had repeatedly robbed his saloons to carry away cases of alcohol. During the trial, Von der Ahe's son Eddie, who was the treasurer of the saloons, testified that his father had routinely sent alcohol to his two mistresses and covered up the loss of inventory with bogus charges of robbery. Unfortunately for Stevenson, he lost the case when he failed to give security for court costs.

Cardinals

13
March

The question of the day: Why did the Browns evict the Cardinals from Sportsman's Park in 1924? In January, the Cardinals failed to make their quarterly rent payment. The Cards claimed it was an oversight and immediately paid upon realizing the error, but Browns owner Phil Ball carried out the eviction proceedings. The real reason for the eviction was the stalled negotiation over who would pay for the expansion of Sportsman's Park. Ball wanted to increase capacity from 18,000 to 32,000 and wanted the Cards to pay part of the cost. Cards owner Sam Breadon refused to spend any money on the improvements. The Cardinals went to court to prevent the eviction, and received a temporary restraining order on March 31 and a permanent one on July 12 that allowed them to remain at the corner of Grand and Dozier. The judge administering the case admonished the Cardinals, however, for the refusal to pay a share of the cost of expanding the ballpark in that it would likely increase the club's profitability. The expansion of the ballpark took place between the 1925 and 1926 seasons.

Cardinals

14
March

A t an auction held at the Old Court-
house in St. Louis on this date in
1899, the Cardinals were sold
to G. A. Gruner for $33,000. Gruner
represented all of the ball club's creditors except St. Louis attorney Edward C.
Becker, who was the only other bidder.
Becker stopped at $31,600. Chris Von
der Ahe's wealth, once estimated at $1 mil-
lion, had vanished by 1899. He owed creditors
thousands of dollars. Von der Ahe had been steadily losing money
for decades on his business ventures, including the Cardinals, while
spending lavishly. A fire that destroyed the Cardinals' ballpark
on April 16, 1898, had sealed his fate. The cost of rebuilding was
$60,000, but insurance covered only about half. Von der Ahe was
also bombarded by lawsuits from many of those injured in the
blaze. Gruner quickly sold the Cardinals to Becker for $40,000 on
March 17. Becker had been acting on behalf of Frank and Stanley
Robison, owner of the Cleveland Spiders, which at the time was
one of the 12 teams in the National League. In 1899, there was no
rule against owning stock in more than one team in baseball. The
Spiders had been one of the best clubs in the NL during the 1890s.
They never won a pennant, but were usually in the thick of the
race. From 1892 through 1898, the Cardinals never finished higher
than ninth place. In 1898, the club had a record of 39-111.

15
March

The question of the day: How did Frank and Stanley Robison transform the Cardinals into winners in 1899?

The Robison brothers, who had amassed a fortune operating streetcars in Cleveland and Fort Wayne, Indiana, failed to turn a profit in baseball, however, because their Cleveland Spiders club was always at or near the bottom of the National League in attendance. Every season from 1892 through 1898, the Cardinals outdrew the Spiders despite putting a vastly inferior product on the field. The Robisons decided on a novel strategy. They would transfer the best of Cleveland's players to St. Louis in an attempt to field a strong club in a better market. Among those they sent from the Spiders to the Cardinals were future Hall of Famers Cy Young, Jesse Burkett and Bobby Wallace. Altogether, the Cardinals received seven of Cleveland's eight starting positions players, the top utility player, and the best two pitchers. The Cardinals, a club with a 39-11 record in 1898, jumped to 84-67 in 1899 with the infusion of new talent. The Spiders, 81-68 in 1898, won only 20 games while losing a major league record 134 times in 1899. At the close of the 1899 season, the NL contracted from 12 teams to eight, and Cleveland was one of the four franchises eliminated.

Cardinals

16 March

The question of the day: How did the Robison brothers fare as owners of the Cardinals after 1899?

After an 84-67 record in 1899, the Cards were just 65-75 in 1900. After the 1900 season, the American League formed as a second major league and began raiding the National League rosters by luring players with higher salaries. The Cardinals were hit hard, losing Cy Young, Jesse Burkett and Bobby Wallace. Worse, Burkett and Wallace signed with the Browns, which became an AL team in 1902. The Cardinals were 580-888 from 1900 through 1909. The winning percentage of .395 was the second worst in the majors during the decade, trailing only the Washington Senators of the American League. Frank Robison was club president until 1906 when he began to lose interest and turned the club over to his brother Stanley. Frank passed away in 1908. Stanley died suddenly of a heart attack in 1911 at the age of 54. His three heirs, a sister, a sister-in-law (Frank's widow) and niece (Frank's daughter) were all women. The niece was Helene Robison Britton, who became the first woman to run a major league team.

17
March

Paul Dean died on this date in 1981. The younger brother (by two years) of Dizzy Dean, Paul was a rookie pitcher in 1934 and won his first seven decisions on the way to a 19-11 record and a 3.43 ERA in a season in which he didn't turn 21 until August. Combined with Dizzy's 30-7 record, the Dean brothers were 49-18 that season as the Cards won the NL pennant. Although the press nicknamed Paul Dean "Daffy" as a gimmick to echo his brother's nickname, Paul was actually shy and serious, unlike the boisterous Dizzy. On September 21, 1934, Dizzy threw a three-hitter for a 13-0 victory in the first game of a doubleheader against the Dodgers at Ebbets Field. He had a no-hitter until Buzz Boyle beat out a slow roller for a single in the eighth inning. Paul followed with a no-hitter in the second tilt for a 3-0 win. He struck out six. The only base runner was Len Koenicke, who walked in the first inning. After that, Paul retired 25 batters in a row. Paul had a 19-12 record in 1935, but developed arm trouble and won only 12 more games, finishing his career at 50-34.

**18
March**

On this date in 1970, Mike Shannon was diagnosed with kidney problems. He had been a player with the club since 1962, starting in right field and later moving to third base. During a routine physical exam during spring training, it was discovered that Shannon suffered from glomerulo-nephritis, a rare disorder that is occasionally fatal. He spent a month in the hospital and was treated at home for another month before being cleared to play. He appeared in 52 games in 1970, batting only .213. Team physician Dr. Stan London announced in mid-August that Shannon's condition had deteriorated, and he wouldn't be allowed to play for the rest of the season. As it turned out, he never played another game. In 1972, he became one of the Cardinals' radio and television broadcasters, a role he still holds. He had no broadcasting experience when he started, and the early years brought him his share of critics, but Cardinals fans today would have a difficult time imagining a game without his unique, passionate style and observations.

19
March

Today's trivia: What is the Cardinals record for most runs scored in a single game in the modern era?

After losing the first game of a doubleheader 10-6 to the Phillies on July 6, 1929, the Cardinals 11th loss in a row, the club exploded in the second game for a 28-6 victory. The 28 runs is a modern NL record and the fourth highest in the majors since 1900. The major league mark is 30 by the Texas Rangers in 30-3 win over the Baltimore Orioles on August 22, 2007. The Cardinals scored ten runs in the first inning, one in the second, two in the fourth and ten in the fifth to take a 23-4 lead. The Cards closed the scoring with five tallies in the eighth. The Phillies pitchers were Jim Willoughby and Elmer Miller, neither of whom retired a batter, Luther Roy (4⅓ innings), and June Green (4⅔ innings). First baseman Jim Bottomley hit a grand slam and drove home six runs. Left fielder Chick Hafey collected five hits, including a grand slam and two doubles, in seven at-bats. Center fielder Taylor Douthit had five singles in six at-bats.

20 March

On this date in 1917, the Cardinals hired 35-year-old Branch Rickey to run the club with the title of president. Rickey was hired away from the St. Louis Browns, where he was business manager. Rickey wanted more control over running a baseball operation than he had with the Browns, and he jumped at the chance to take over the Cardinals. Branch Wesley Rickey was born in 1881, the son of a poor farmer in Lucasville, Ohio. Raised by strict Methodist parents who scrimped and saved for his education, Rickey attended Ohio Wesleyan University, and graduated 1½ years ahead of schedule. He caught the attention of major league scouts, and played 118 games as a catcher with the Browns and Yankees from 1905 through 1907. After his playing days ended, Rickey attended the University of Michigan Law School and earned a degree by squeezing a three-year course of study into two years while coaching the baseball team. Building baseball's first extensive farm system, Rickey ran the Cardinals front office for 25 years and transformed one of the worst operations in baseball into a dynasty that would win nine NL pennants and six world championships from 1926 through 1946.

Cardinals

21
March

Joe Medwick died on this date in 1975 at age 63. A member of the Hall of Fame, "Ducky" played for the Cardinals from 1932 through 1940 and again in 1947 and '48. Perhaps his most famous "oddball" day was game seven of the 1934 World Series against the Tigers in Detroit. The game was played on October 9. The drama appeared to be over quickly as the Cards jumped on Eldon Auker for seven runs in the third inning and added two more in the sixth to make the score 9-0. During the inning, Medwick slid hard into third baseman Marv Owen on a triple. Medwick knocked down Owen who stepped on Medwick's shin as he fell. As both lay on the ground, Medwick kicked Owen in the chest. They scrambled to their feet to fight, but were separated before blows could be struck. When Medwick took his position in left field in the bottom of the sixth, he was pelted with bottles and garbage by angry Detroit fans. He went to the field three times and retreated to the dugout on each occasion under a barrage of refuse. Efforts to quell the fans proved futile, and faced with the possibility of a riot with the Cardinals holding an almost insurmountable lead, commissioner Kenesaw Landis removed Medwick from the game "for his own safety." The delay lasted 17 minutes, and Chick Fullis took Medwick's place in left field.

Cardinals

22
March

On this date in 2007, Cardinals manager Tony La Russa caused a minor scandal in the organization when he was arrested in Jupiter, Florida, for drunk driving. According to the police, La Russa was found asleep at the wheel of his car while stopped at an intersection after midnight. La Russa was awakened by police officers and denied being intoxicated, but he failed sobriety tests and was arrested. He was found to have a blood alcohol content of .093 above the .08 legal limit in Florida. La Russa pled guilty later in the year and was sentenced to community service and attendance at a DUI school. The organization stood by the long-time manager, making a public statement that the situation would be handled in house.

Cardinals

23
March

Happy Birthday, Homer Smoot, who was born on this date in 1878. As a Cardinal outfielder on July 1, 1903, Smoot hit into a "quadruple" play during a 5-2 loss to the Giants in New York. Smoot hit a fly ball caught by center fielder Roger Bresnahan with the bases loaded. Bresnahan threw to catcher John Warner to retire Clarence Currie trying to score from third for the second out. Warner then fired the ball to shortstop George Davis to nail Patsy Donovan attempting to advance from first to second for the third out. Even though the inning was over, neither team seemed to realize it, and play continued. Davis saw John Farrell, who started the play as the base runner on second, trying to score, and he instinctively threw home. Warned tagged Farrell for the "fourth out" of the inning.

Cardinals

24
March

Bobby Slaybaugh, a 20-year-old pitching prospect, suffered the loss of his right eye as a result of being struck in the face by a line drive during spring training in St. Petersburg, Florida. Slaybaugh, a strikeout artist with strong potential, was pitching batting practice when a drive by Jim Dickey hit him, shattering the left cheekbone, forcing the eyeball partly out of the socket. Efforts to save the eye were unsuccessful, and it was removed April 3. Slaybaugh pitched in the minors three months later, but never reached the big leagues. He retired in 1954.

Cardinals

25
March

The question of the day: Why were the Cardinals in the Eastern Division from 1969 through 1993?

In defiance of geographic logic, the Cardinals and Cubs were in the Eastern Division while the Reds and Braves were in the West from 1969 through 1993. The divisions were created with the expansion of the National League from ten teams to 12. The Cards were placed in the East because of the shortsightedness of Mets chairman of the board M. Donald Grant. In 1968, the three biggest road draws were the Dodgers, Giants and Cardinals, and Grant insisted that the Mets be in the same division as one of the three. Being the easternmost of those three teams, St. Louis moved into the Eastern Division, but the Cardinals would agree only if long-standing rival Chicago were included. That put Atlanta and Cincinnati, two cities east of St. Louis and Chicago, into the west. The Cardinals were NL champions in 1964, 1967 and 1968, but shortly after division play began the club declined to relative mediocrity while the Reds became one of the top attractions in baseball.

Cardinals

26
March

On this date in 1966, a model of the new scoreboard to be installed at Busch Memorial Stadium, set to open on May 12, was unveiled to the public. Able to show only four colors and lacking animation, the original scoreboard at the second Busch Stadium seems quaint by today's standards, but it was cutting edge at a time when there were few electronic scoreboards of its size in the country. The scoreboard was in two units, each measuring 145 feet long and 21 feet high. The left field unit carried the stats of the game in progress along with advertisements and public service announcements. The right field section displayed out-of-town contests and the message board. On the right field side, a neon Cardinal streaked across each time a St. Louis player hit a home run. The "flight" was accompanied by an actual studio recording of a redbird's chirp. At the same time, on the left field portion, an eagle flapping its wings was superimposed over Anheuser-Busch's trademark "A." The original scoreboard was replaced in 1983.

Cardinals

27
March

Happy Birthday, Miller Huggins, who was born on this date in 1878. He was a second baseman for the Cardinals from 1910 through 1916 and the manager from 1913 through 1917. On May 4, 1913, he used outfielder Ted Cather and first baseman Ed Konetchy as pitchers during a 13-inning, 10-8 win over the Cubs in Chicago. After Cather pitched one-third of an inning and gave up two runs, Konetchy went 4⅔ innings, allowed no runs and one hit while striking out three, and was the winning pitcher. The Cardinals trailed 6-2 before scoring six runs in the ninth inning, but allowed two runs in the bottom of the inning to knot the contest at 8-8 when Konetchy was called in with one out. Huggins turned to Cather and Konetchy because he took only three pitchers to Chicago. The Cards played in Pittsburgh on Saturday May 3, in Chicago on May 4, and after an off day on May 5, started a road trip in Philadelphia on May 6. The unusual scheduling was set up because Sunday baseball was illegal in Pennsylvania and the Cards traveled to Chicago rather than sit idle on a day of the week that usually drew the largest crowds. Huggins didn't believe he needed more than three pitchers in the May 4 contest in Chicago, so he sent the rest of the staff to Philadelphia to save on train fare.

28
March

On this date in 1935, Cards owner Sam Breadon stated that he might move the Cardinals to Detroit, but that there was no immediate prospect of the shift. Breadon was concerned because of low attendance figures for Cardinals games at Sportsman's Park. In 1934, with one of the most colorful clubs in history and one that won a pennant on the final day of the season, the Cards drew only 325,056 at home, the fifth-best figure in the NL and the tenth-best in the majors. The average home attendance for clubs in the big leagues in 1934 was 435,232. The Cardinals attendance improved to 506,084 in 1935.

29
March

On this date in 1913, the Cardinals lost most of their equipment in a flood in Indianapolis. The uniforms, bats, gloves and shoes were destroyed. The gear was located at Washington Park in Indianapolis, where the Cardinals were scheduled to play exhibition games for a week. None of the games were played because of rain and subsequent floods that put the ballpark under ten feet of water. Moreover, the Cards were marooned in Indianapolis and were unable to even practice because all highways and railroads out of the city were swamped in the massive flooding, which caused 467 deaths and left 200,000 homeless in Indiana and Ohio.

Cardinals

30
March

The question of the day: How did Garry Templeton create controversy in spring training in 1979?

During a radio interview with Mike Shannon, Templeton said he was going to play "conservatively" during the upcoming season and demanded to be traded. The Cardinals shortstop was upset after receiving a pay cut during the previous off-season. "I'm not going to play hard," Templeton said. "I'm not going to do my best." One newspaper quoted Templeton saying, "For an extra $30,000, I'll play like they never saw before." In addition to his contract, Templeton was angry that the Cardinals were trying to change his style of play on defense after leading major league shortstops in errors with 40 in 1978. Templeton later apologized for his remarks and that season he hit .314 with 211 hits, 105 runs, 26 stolen bases, nine homers, and a league-leading 20 triples. The triples total is the highest of any Cardinal since Stan Musial hit 20 in 1946. Templeton is the only National Leaguer to lead the league in triples three years in a row. He also gave back to the community by purchasing 50 box seats for every summer game for underprivileged and handicapped children.

Cardinals

31
March

On this date in 1993, the Cardinals traded Mark Clark and Juan Andujar to the Indians for Mark Whiten. In the best single-game performance in Cardinals history, Whiten hit four homers and drove in 12 runs, both of which tied major league records, during a 15-2 victory over the Reds in the second game of a twilight doubleheader at Riverfront Stadium. Whiten hit a sacrifice fly in the first game, won by Cincinnati 14-13 with two runs in the ninth inning. The two runs scored on a fly ball that Whiten, playing right field, misplayed into a triple. In the first inning of the second game, Whiten hit a 408-foot, opposite-field homer off Larry Luebbers to left field on a 2-0 pitch. It was Whiten's first homer since August 11, a span of 80 at-bats. After a fly ball out to third base in the fourth, he hit a 397-foot, three-run blast to right-center field on the first pitch from Mike Anderson. Whiten connected off Anderson again in the seventh with two runners on base on a 2-1 pitch that traveled 388 feet and cleared the right field wall. In the ninth, Whiten hit a 441-foot shot to right-center against Rob Dibble. When Whiten hit the final home run, at about 1:00 a.m. Cincinnati time, there were only about 2,000 fans left in the ballpark. A switch-hitter, Whiten hit all four homers from the left side of the plate.

Cardinals

April

Cardinals

01
April

Today's trivia: How many players have hit four homers in a game? Through the close of the 2010 campaign, there have been only 15 players who have hit four homers in a game. Whiten is the only Cardinal to perform the feat. He was the first Cardinal to hit more than three homers in a game since Reggie Smith clubbed three in 1976. It didn't happen again until Mark McGwire collected three in a game in 1998. Whiten finished his career, which he spent with eight clubs over 11 seasons, with 105 homers. Of the 15 players who hit four homers in a game, the only ones with fewer homers are Bobby Lowe (71), Pat Seerey (86) and Ed Delahanty (101). Whiten's 12 RBIs in the game tied the major league record set by Jim Bottomley of the Cardinals in 1924. Whiten's 13 RBIs in the doubleheader tied the mark set by Nate Colbert of the Padres in 1972.

Cardinals

02
April

On this date in 1937, Dizzy Dean and Joe Medwick got into a fight with reporters in the lobby of the Tampa Terrace Hotel in Tampa, Florida. Dean started the fray by confronting *New York Daily News* columnist Jack Miley over an article that claimed Dean's wife Pat "wore the pants of the family." Dean and Miley traded roundhouse swings. Irving Kupcinet of the *Chicago Daily News*, who had played in the NFL with the Philadelphia Eagles as recently as 1935, tried to intervene and was punched by Medwick. Kupcinet sprawled backward into a potted palm tree that started a chain reaction knocking down floor lamps, plants, and four other palms. Miley was struck in the forehead by the spiked shoe of an unidentified Cardinal player and sported a cut on his scalp. Kupcinet suffered a black eye. Dean and Medwick apologized and promised never to strike a sportswriter again.

Cardinals

03
April

The question of the day: Which Cardinal pitcher had the greatest season?

Cardinal pitchers have posted some great seasons through the years, but it's tough to top Bob Gibson in 1968. His 1.12 earned run average is the lowest of anyone in the majors with a minimum of 150 innings pitched from 1915 through the present. Gibson's 13 shutouts that year are the most by any pitcher since Grover Alexander recorded 16 for the Phillies in 1916. Gibson completed 28 of his 34 starts. He was lifted for a pinch-hitter in the other six starts. In June, Gibson pitched five consecutive shutouts in which he allowed 21 hits, walked five, and struck out 35 in 45 innings. During a stretch in June and July, he surrendered only one run over 71 innings. In ten straight starts from June 6 through July 25, Gibson pitched eight shutouts. Over a span of 105 consecutive innings from June 2 through August 4, he gave up only three runs. Gibson finished the year with a record of 22-9, however, because of a lack of run support. The club averaged 3.6 runs per game that year. Had the Cardinals maintained that modest figure in each of his starts, Gibson would have been 30-4 in 1968, and would have had a 19-game winning streak from April through July.

Cardinals

04
April

The question of the day: How did the Cardinals win a game by forfeit in 1995?

The Cardinals won by forfeit over the Dodgers in Los Angeles on August 10. With one out in the bottom of the ninth and the Cards leading 2-1, the umpires stopped the game after some in the raucous sellout crowd of 53,361 on Ball Night littered the field with balls for the third time. The game was previously delayed six minutes in the top of the seventh, and again in the ninth after Dodger outfielder Raul Mondesi and manager Tommy Lasorda were ejected after Mondesi struck out. The umpires ordered the Cardinals to leave the field while the balls were picked up. After another delay of five minutes, the Cards went back on the field and a few more balls were thrown. One just missed hitting center fielder Brian Jordan in the head. At that point, the umpires called the game. It was the first forfeit in the major leagues since 1979, and the first in the National League since 1954.

05
April

On this date in 1974, the Cardinals scored two runs in the tenth inning and defeat the Pirates 6-5 on Opening Day before 24,210 at Busch Memorial Stadium. The game ended in bizarre fashion. The Cards went to bat in the bottom of the tenth inning trailing 5-4. With no outs, singles by Bake McBride, Ken Reitz and Tim McCarver produced the tying run. Jose Cruz followed with a safe bunt, loading the bases. Lou Brock lined to right field, where Gene Clines trapped the ball. The runners held, fearing the ball would be caught, and Jim Dwyer, running for Reitz, was easily forced out on Clines's throw to catcher Mike Ryan. Ryan threw to Richie Hebner at third, forcing McCarver, who had retreated to second. Hebner threw to second baseman Rennie Stennett, who tagged McCarver instead of stepping on second, which would have forced out Cruz for a triple play. While the Pirates were arguing with the umpires that Stennett had touched the bag, Cruz pushed on to second. Ted Sizemore then singled to drive in Cruz with the winning run.

Cardinals

06
April

On this date in 2001, Albert Pujols hit his first career homer. It was struck off Armando Reynoso in the fourth inning of a 12-9 win over the Diamondbacks in Phoenix. When spring training began, Pujols was 21 years old and virtually unknown, even in St. Louis. He had not only never appeared in a big league game, he also played just one season as a professional and only 24 games above the Class A level. Despite his lack of experience, Pujols responded with one of the greatest rookie seasons in baseball history. Playing in 161 games, he hit .329 with 194 hits, 37 home runs, 47 doubles, 130 RBIs and 112 runs scored. Pujols established rookie records for RBIs, total bases (360) and extra base hits (88). He also played all over the field in 2001, appearing in 55 games at third base, 42 at first, 39 in left field and 39 in right. Pujols was the NL Rookie of the Year and finished fourth in the MVP voting. Through the 2010 season, Pujols won three MVP awards (2005, 2008 and 2009), finished second four times (2002, 2003, 2006 and 2010) and third once (2004).

Cardinals

07
April

The question of the day: What Cardinals manager previously was an umpire?

Team owner Chris Von der Ahe surprised Cardinal fans by hiring Tim Hurst as manager in 1898. Prior to his appointment, Hurst had been a National League umpire from 1891 through 1897, in addition to serving as an official at numerous running, walking and bicycle races and boxing and wrestling matches. A former coal miner in Pennsylvania, he had a reputation for being able to tame the rowdy players of the day. Hurst often settled disputes by striking disgruntled players with his fists or his mask. In 1897, an irate fan in Cincinnati tossed a beer stein at him. Hurst threw it back, hit another fan, and was arrested. It was hoped that Hurst's toughness would rub off on the Cardinals, who were 29-102 in 1897, but the club compiled a 39-111 record in 1898, and he was fired at the end of the season. As an example of his honesty and integrity, Hurst actually umpired two Cardinals games during that season, with the approval of the opposition, when the regular umpire failed to show up. He obviously showed no favoritism as the Cards lost both games.

Cardinals

08
April

On this date in 1891, the Cardinals opened the season with a 7-7 tie, called after nine innings by darkness, against Cincinnati at Sportsman's Park. The umpire (there was only one on the field in 1891) was ex-Cardinal Bill Gleason, whose calls were so impartial that the partisan St. Louis fans jeered him even though most of his decisions favored the local club. Cincinnati manager King Kelly was naturally incensed. When the ninth inning started, it was so dark that it was next to impossible to see the ball. Still, Gleason ordered that play continue into the tenth. The Cardinals quickly scored in the top of the inning (at the time the home team had the option of batting first), and Cincinnati began to stall, hoping the inning wouldn't be completed and the score would revert to the 7-7 tie at the end of the ninth. When Gleason refused to halt the contest, Kelly pulled his team off the field. The umpire declared a forfeit in favor of St. Louis. Cardinals owner Chris Von Der Ahe protested the forfeit, claiming his club would rather win on its own merits and not because of an incompetent umpire. Gleason was so abysmal that the American Association fired him after one game.

Cardinals

09
April

On this date in 1953, Cardinals owner August Busch, who bought the franchise on February 20, purchased Sportsman's Park from the St. Louis Browns. The price was $800,000. Busch then leased the ballpark back to the Browns for $175,000 per season. Busch immediately announced that he was changing the name of the ballpark to Budweiser Stadium after his brewery's signature beer. The name Sportsman's Park had been associated with baseball in St. Louis since 1866. The change to Budweiser Stadium drew fire from temperance groups and other organizations, as well as other NL owners, objecting to naming the facility after an alcoholic beverage. A day later, Busch changed the name of his new ballpark to Busch Stadium. (A year later, the company introduced a new product called Busch Bavarian Beer.) It was the first of three Cardinals homes named Busch Stadium. By 1995, sentiments had changed over naming a ballpark after a beer, as there were few objections over naming the home of the Colorado Rockies Coors Field. The Browns were Busch's tenants for less than six months. After the 1953 season concluded, the franchise moved to Baltimore, where it was renamed the Orioles.

Cardinals

**10
April**

The third ballpark named Busch Stadium opened on this date in 2006. The Cardinals defeated the Brewers 6-4 before 41,936. The ceremonial first pitches were thrown by Chris Carpenter and Albert Pujols to Bob Gibson and Willie McGee. Brady Clark was the first batter, and on the second pitch from Mark Mulder, lined to second baseman Aaron Miles. The first hit was a single by Milwaukee's Carlos Lee in the second inning. One batter later, Bill Hall homered. The Cards tied the score 2-2 in the third with the first run recorded on a home run by Albert Pujols. A two-run double by Scott Rolen in the fourth put the Cardinals into the lead. Mark Mulder went eight innings and contributed a double in the fifth inning and a single in the seventh. They were the first two extra-base hits of his career. The stadium opened about 5,000 seats short of capacity because the left field section was not yet completed. The entire ballpark opened for use on May 29. Statues of St. Louis baseball greats that surrounded the old stadium were moved to the corner of Clark and Eighth Streets. Included are Stan Musial, Bob Gibson, Jack Buck, Lou Brock, Red Schoendienst, Enos Slaughter, Dizzy Dean, Rogers Hornsby, George Sisler and James "Cool Papa" Bell.

Cardinals

11
April

The question of the day: When was the last time the Cardinals experienced three consecutive losing seasons?

The Cardinals haven't experienced a long losing stretch in more than a half-century. The last time the club had three losing seasons in a row was in 1954, 1955 and 1956. The 1956 team just missed the .500 mark with a 76-78 record. Prior to 1954-56, the Cardinals hadn't ended the season below .500 at least three years in a row since compiling nine losing years in succession from 1902 through 1910. The Cardinals and the Dodgers are the only franchises in the majors that haven't had at least one stretch of three straight losing seasons since 1985. The last time it happened to the Dodgers was five in a row from 1933 through 1937 when the club was located in Brooklyn. The Cardinals have gone longer than anyone else without a period of four or more losing seasons.

Cardinals

12
April

After ten seasons in the American Association, the Cardinals played their first game in the National League on this date in 1892. The Cards lost 14-10 to Chicago in front of a crowd of 10,000 at Sportsman's Park. The Cubs led 7-1 in the fifth inning and 14-5 in the seventh before allowing St. Louis back in the game. In his first game as a Cardinal, Cliff Carroll hit a home run. The day began with an extravagant morning parade that started at Sportsman's Park, moved down Grand to Washington, and proceeded to the Lindell Hotel and back through the principal streets to the ballpark. A marching band led the procession, which included carriages toting world champion boxer John L. Sullivan, Chicago manager Cap Anson, celebrated actress Lillian Russell, Missouri Governor Dave Francis, and St. Louis Mayor Edward Noonan. The two teams entered Sportsman's Park with a brass band leading the way.

Cardinals

13
April

On this date in 1974, in the seventh game of the season, Lou Brock stole his first two bases of the year during a 6-4 win over the Pirates in Pittsburgh. When the 1974 campaign began, Brock had led the NL in steals seven times, runs twice, and doubles and triples once each, and had four seasons of 200 or more hits. He had also played in three World Series. He was bothered, however, by what he believed was a lack of respect for his accomplishments. He had been named to only three All-Star teams, and his highest finish in the MVP voting was sixth in 1968 and 1973. Although he was due to turn 35 in August 1974, and had never stolen more than 74 bases in a season, Brock set out to break Maury Wills's single-season stolen base record of 104, set in 1962. With the record, Brock felt he would receive the recognition he deserved. Prior to 1974, Brock had never attempted more than 92 steals in a season. In 1974, he swiped 118 in 151 attempts. He batted .304, scored 105 runs, and collected 194 hits. After setting the new record, Brock dropped to 56 in both 1975 and 1976. Rickey Henderson stole 130 bases in 1982 to pass Brock as the single-season record holder, though Brock still has the National League mark and the second highest figure in the modern era.

14
April

Today's trivia: Which Cardinal player compiled MLB's highest single-season batting average (minimum 500 plate appearances) from 1902 through the present?

Second baseman Rogers Hornsby batted .424 for the Cardinals in 1924 with 227 hits in 536 at-bats. Among his hits were 43 doubles, 14 triples and 25 home runs. Hornsby won six NL batting titles in a row in St. Louis from 1920 through 1925 with averages of .370 in 1920, .397 in 1921, .401 in 1922, .384 in 1923, .424 in 1924 and .403 in 1925. From 1921 through 1925, Hornsby batted .402. No one over a five-year stretch in major league history has hit .400 or better. Hornsby not only batted over .400 in both 1922 and 1925, but led the NL in home runs as well. He clouted 42 in 1922 and 39 in 1925. Hornsby's 450 total bases in 1922 are the second highest in baseball history, behind only Babe Ruth's 457 in 1921. Hornsby could maintain hot streaks that are almost impossible to comprehend. From July 4 through July 20, 1923, he had 40 hits in 68 at-bats for an average of .588. From August 20 through August 29, 1925 Hornsby and the Cardinals played 14 games in just ten days, yet he collected 34 hits in 51 at-bats, a batting average of .667.

15
April

On this date in 1972, the Cardinals traded Jerry Reuss to the Astros for Scipio Spinks and Lance Clemons. Reuss was a 22-year-old left-handed pitcher who angered August Busch by holding out for a higher salary than the Cardinals owner was willing to pay. Reuss also caused consternation among the club hierarchy by growing a beard. Busch ordered Reuss to shave it off. He refused. Busch ordered general manager Bing Devine to trade Reuss, a native of St. Louis. After the trade, Reuss won 198 more big-league games. Spinks had three distinctions as a Redbird. First was his unusual first name. Spinks was named, as were generations of men in the family, for the Roman general who conquered Hannibal and burned Carthage. Secondly, Spinks carried a stuffed gorilla he named "Mighty Joe Young" everywhere he went for good luck. Finally, after running through the third base coach's stop sign, Spinks suffered a severe knee injury sliding into Johnny Bench on a game against the Reds on July 4, 1972. Spinks had a 1-5 record after hurting his knee and was only 25 when he pitched his last major league game.

Cardinals

16
April

On this date in 1898, a fire destroyed almost all of New Sportsman's Park during a game against the Cubs. The ballpark, made entirely of wood, was crowded with 6,000 people. The Cubs had just gone onto the field in the second inning when a small column of smoke ascended from the lower corner of the northwest section of the grandstand. As the fire spread, there was a rush for the front of the stands, and fans jumped onto the playing field, a distance of 12 feet, and stampeded toward the four staircases at the rear of the ballpark. Within three minutes, the roof caught fire. When spectators surged toward the exit between the clubhouse and the saloon, they found the gate closed. The crowd formed a huge battering ram to crash through the barrier. The players of both teams rescued many fans. No one was killed, but at least 100 were burned, and many had broken limbs. The flames also spread to an adjacent railway depot and the fairgrounds across the street. The only part of the ballpark left standing was the right field bleachers. Club owner Chris Von Der Ahe lost all of his personal effects, including trophies and correspondence files. Insurance covered only part of the loss. He had also taken out thousands of dollars in loans for improvements to the ballpark, carried out during the previous off-season, only to see it all go up in smoke.

Cardinals

17
April

A day after a fire destroyed most of the ballpark (see April 16), an exhausted group of Cardinals made 11 errors and lost 14-1 to the Cubs at New Sportsman's Park on this date in 1898. Chris Von Der Ahe was not about to lose an attractive Sunday date, and with the help of electric lights, he assembled a group of carpenters to clear the debris and put up 1,700 temporary seats overnight. He ordered his players to join the construction crew. A crowd of 7,500 attended the game, lured by the spring weather and a curiosity to see the ruins. Most of the fans stood behind ropes strung behind the outfield. Kid Carsey pitched two innings before the fire the previous day, then spent the evening hours unloading lumber for the rebuilding project. He started the April 17 contest and allowed one run over the first three innings before Cubs batters used their lumber to score ten runs in the fourth. A homestand of about a dozen games was transferred to other cities while New Sportsman's Park was rebuilt. It was completed by July 4. This configuration lasted only three years. It was destroyed by another fire in 1901.

Cardinals

18
April

On the date in 1987, Tom Herr hit a walk-off grand slam to climax a five-run tenth inning, lifting the Cards to a 12-8 win over the Mets. Jesse Orosco gave up the homer. It was "Seat Cushion Night" at Busch Stadium and fans showed their appreciation for the victory by tossing thousands of the cushions onto the field as Herr rounded the bases. He drove in six runs in the game and showed nimble footwork in dodging the flying cushions and tip-toeing around those that landed in the basepaths. Herr drove in 83 runs on the season, the second-highest RBI total of his career.

19
April

The question of the day: What was unusual about Larry Jaster's 1966 season?

In 1966, Larry Jaster threw five shutouts, and all five were against the Dodgers. They were also the first five shutouts of his career. Only two other pitchers since 1900 have recorded five shutouts over one team in a season, none since 1916, and Jaster is the only one with five consecutive shutouts over one club. There are many oddities to Jaster's accomplishment. He entered the season with a 3-0 record, was 11-5 in 1966, but only 19-28 afterward before his career ended in 1972. Jaster pitched only two more shutouts in the majors after 1966. In the five shutouts versus Los Angeles, Jaster allowed only 24 hits, each of them singles, in 45 innings. The Dodgers also won the NL pennant in 1966. Against the other eight NL clubs that season, Jaster pitched 106⅔ innings and had an ERA of 4.64. His ineffectiveness also led to a trip to the minors. Jaster spent six weeks in May and June of the 1966 season with Tulsa in the Pacific Coast League. While in the minors, Jaster missed a June series against the Dodgers, posted a 2-4 record with a 4.98 ERA, and failed to pitch a shutout.

Cardinals

20
April

On this date in 1908, Bugs Raymond pitched a one-hitter, but lost 2-0 to the Cubs in St. Louis. Both runs scored in the sixth inning on two walks, an error, and a single by Harry Steinfeldt on a questionable scoring decision. Pitching in his first full season in 1908 at the age of 26, Raymond had a 2.03 ERA but posted a 15-25 record because of hard-luck losses like this one. The Cardinals were shutout 11 times when he pitched. An out-of-control drunk, his alcoholism led to numerous escapades, constant trouble, and the end of a promising career by 1911. Although his career was relatively short, Raymond earned a lasting reputation as one of the sport's most humorous characters. On one occasion, he showed a waiter how to throw a curveball by throwing a beer glass through a plate glass window. To deter Raymond's ardor for alcohol, managers tried fines and sending paychecks directly to his wife so he wouldn't have any money for drink. Raymond responded by trading baseballs for bottles of beer. In September 1912, Raymond was found dead in a hotel room in Chicago of a cerebral hemorrhage. During the previous month, he was involved in two drunken brawls. In one, he was hit repeatedly with a baseball bat in a barroom altercation, and in another was kicked in the head in a fight during an amateur baseball game.

Cardinals

21
April

The question of the day: How did pitcher Stu Miller fare in his first three major league appearances? In his major league debut on August 17, 1952, Stu Miller pitched the Cardinals to a 1-0 victory over the Cubs at Wrigley Field. Miller allowed six hits and closed out the game by striking out Bill Serena with runners on first and third. In his next start on August 17, Miller came within one out of pitching his second shutout in a row before closing out a 2-1 victory over the Reds at Sportsman's Park. The lone Cincinnati run scored in the ninth inning on two errors by shortstop Solly Hemus. Miller turned in his third brilliant start in his third big league game on August 22, beating the Giants 3-1 in St. Louis. The lone New York run crossed the plate in the eighth inning. Miller allowed no earned runs in his first 25 big league innings. He failed to maintain his success, however, and was traded to the Phillies in May 1956. Miller later became one of the top relievers in baseball during the 1960s as a member of the San Francisco Giants and Baltimore Orioles.

Cardinals

22
April

The Cardinals defeat the Louisville Colonels during a quarrelsome afternoon at Sportsman's Park on this date in 1888. At the time, umpires had the power to levy fines. Umpire Jack McQuaid fined Louisville second baseman Reddy Mack for profanity and ordered him to the bench. Mack refused to leave and was fined several more times. McQuaid called for the St. Louis police to remove Mack, and three officers took hold of the Louisville player. Louisville outfielder Hub Collins grabbed a bat and ordered Mack's release. The police let go of him, but the game was delayed 20 minutes while Mack continued to jaw with McQuaid. Play resumed after Mack was allowed to remain in the game.

Cardinals

23
April

On this date in 1999, Cardinals third baseman Fernando Tatis became the only player in major league history to hit two grand slams in a single inning during a 12-5 win over the Dodgers in Los Angeles. Tatis also set a major league mark for most RBIs during with inning with eight. Previously, no one had more than six in an inning. Tatis hit both slams in an 11-run third inning off Chan Ho Park. Tatis's first slam came with the Cardinals trailing 2-0 on a 2-0 pitch with no outs. Tatis faced Park again with the bases loaded and two outs later in the third, and homered into the left field pavilion on a 3-2 pitch. The home run outburst came in Tatis's 226th big league game. He had only 24 prior home runs. None of them was a grand slam, and Tatis had only one previous multi-homer came in 1997 as a Texas Ranger. Through 2009, only 15 players have hit two grand slams in a game. The only others in the NL are Atlanta Braves pitcher Tony Cloninger in 1966 and Josh Willingham of the Nationals in 2009. Tatis is also the only Cardinals player with two home runs in an inning.

Cardinals

24 April

The question of the day: Who was Helene Britton?

Helene Britton inherited ownership of the Cardinals in March 1911 after her uncle, Stanley Robison, died of a heart attack at the age of 54. Fellow National League owners did not want a woman running the Cardinals. This was 1911, and women did not even have the right to vote at the time. Britton was also only 32 years old with no prior experience running a business. At Robison's funeral, NL owners, some of whom were pallbearers, tried to persuade the grieving family to sell the club. The family ignored the pleas, and four days after Stanley's death, it was announced that Britton would assume control of the Cardinals. She would also become the first woman to own a professional team in any sport. A militant advocate for woman's rights, Britton took an active role in running the club and attended every major league meeting, much to the discomfort of her fellow owners. Known as "Lady Bee," she had been raised around baseball with a father and uncle owning two big league clubs in Cleveland and St. Louis.

Cardinals

25
April

The question of the day: How did Helene Britton fare as owner of the Cardinals?

Like most pioneering woman, Britton had to undergo a great deal of chauvinism, particularly in a male-dominated profession like baseball, and struggled to gain the respect of her managers, players, and the sportswriters who covered the club. In addition, Mrs. Britton lacked the financial resources to compete with the other teams in the league and needed either a new ballpark or a massive rebuilding of League Park, which she renamed Robison Field in 1912 in honor of her family. In 1916, Helene and her husband Schuyler divorced. By that time, she had grown weary of owning the Cardinals. Losing teams and new competition from the Federal League had strained her cash reserves. There was also a probability that the United States would be involved in World War I, which added to her uncertainty over the future. She sold the franchise to a group headed by James Jones in March 1917. She remarried and moved to Philadelphia. She died in 1950.

26
April

The question of the day: If the Cardinals had won the 1927 National League pennant, where would the World Series have been played?

The Cardinals finished second to the Pirates in the 1927 NL pennant race just 1½ games out of first. Had the Cards appeared in the World Series that year, the club might not have been able to play in St. Louis. On September 29, a tornado ripped through the city resulting in 87 deaths. Some 500 more people were injured in a path of devastation that covered six square miles on both sides of the Mississippi River. At Sportsman's Park, the twister flipped the pavilion roof onto Grand Avenue, bent the flagpole in center field, and scattered debris all over the ballpark. The Cards played their final home game as scheduled on October 1, but had the club reached the Fall Classic, the expensive damage to Sportsman's Park probably would have prompted moving the event out of St. Louis since it would have been difficult to make repairs necessary to handle capacity crowds. Many major traffic arteries near the ballpark were also closed.

Cardinals

27
April

On this date in 1893, the Cardinals opened New Sportsman's Park with a 4-2 win over Louisville with a crowd of 12,000. Cards hurler Pink Hawley took a no-hitter into the ninth inning before emerging with the win. The ballpark was located on the southeast corner of Vandeveter and Natural Bridge across from Fairgrounds Park. To celebrate the opening of the new facility, a parade was staged. According to newspaper reports, "There were in line a sufficient number of carriages to cover more than three blocks." The vehicles contained state and city officials, prominent citizens, officers and directors of the Cardinals club, and players from the St. Louis and Louisville teams. One of the carriages was led by four of Adolph Busch's finest black Arabian horses with Busch himself handling the reins. The Italian-American cavalry and two brass bands furnished the music along the route. Many of the buildings in the city were decorated with flags and flowers and bunting adorned New Sportsman's Park. Two bands that had taken part in the parade played 53 pieces of music in an hour-long ceremony prior to the game. A ceremony was held in which souvenirs and copies of the daily newspapers were buried in a time capsule under home plate. There were nearly 2,000 women present, "dressed in their latest and prettiest spring finery."

Cardinals

28
April

The question of the day: What did New Sportsman's Park look like when it opened in 1893?

New Sportsman's Park had an enormous playing field. It was 470 feet down the left field foul line, 520 to the deepest part of left-center, 500 to straightaway center, 330 to right-center and 290 down the right field line. The backstop was 120 feet from home plate. The field was ringed by a bicycle track for races. There were 14,500 seats at the ballpark, which was constructed entirely of wood. Streetcar service brought fans right to the main gate after club owner Chris Von der Ahe gave the Lindell Railway 200 feet of land for a loop. There were private boxes, a clubhouse, a pavilion, a rooftop press box, and a ladies' powder room. A long bar located on the ground floor sold beer and sandwiches for a nickel. A horseracing track was added in 1895. New Sportsman's Park burned down in 1898, but the Cardinals continued to play at the corner of Vandeveter and Natural Bridge until 1920. Beaumont High School is currently located on the site. Among Beaumont's graduates is Hall of Fame manager Earl Weaver (Class of 1948).

Cardinals

29
April

On this date in 2007, Cardinals pitcher Josh Hancock was killed in a car accident at 12:35 a.m. on a St. Louis highway. He had been with the club since the start of the 2006 season. Hancock was killed on impact when his Ford Explorer hit a tow truck that was parked on the left westbound lane of Highway 40. The truck was parked with its emergency lights flashing behind a disabled car. The truck driver was not injured. A police report revealed that Hancock was intoxicated at the time of the accident with an alcohol level nearly twice the legal limit. It was the second in-season death of a Cardinals player in five years. The other was Darryl Kile in 2002 (see June 22). The Cardinals-Cubs game scheduled for April 29 at Busch Stadium was postponed. The Cardinals uniforms included a black circular patch with his number 32 for the rest of the season.

30
April

Rookie first baseman Rocky Nelson hit a bizarre "inside the glove" home run for the Cardinals on this date in 1949 in the ninth inning of a 4-3 win over the Cubs at Wrigley Field. With Chicago leading 3-2, two outs, and a Cardinal runner on base, Nelson hit a fly ball to the outfield. Cubs center fielder Andy Pafko believed he had made a diving somersault catch off his shoe-tops for what he believed was the final out. Pafko ran toward the dugout with the ball. Second base umpire Al Barlick, in a delayed call, ruled that Pafko had trapped it. Pafko, ignoring his teammates' frantic pleas to throw the ball, headed for the umpire to protests the decision while Nelson circled the bases as the ball was inside Pafko's glove. Pafko finally made a belated throw home when Nelson was only a few steps from home plate, and the Cardinal batter was safe with what would prove to be the game-winning run. The Cubs' arguing delayed the game for ten minutes and the crowd of 30,775 showed its disapproval by showering the field with debris.

Cardinals

May

Cardinals

01
May

On this date in 1891, the Cardinals won 3-1 despite collecting only one hit off Cincinnati's Frank Dwyer in Cincinnati. Dummy Hoy recorded the only hit, a pop-up that landed for a single just behind third base in the fourth inning. The hit by Hoy didn't figure in the scoring, however. The Cardinals scored two runs in the first and one in the second with the benefit of walks and errors. William "Dummy" Hoy was deaf, stood only five-foot-six and weighed just 160 pounds, but he played in the major leagues from 1888 through 1902. The 1891 season was his only one in St. Louis. Many histories called him a "deaf-mute," but he learned a few phrases to help him in his profession, such as "You are rotten" which he directed at umpires who displeased him. Hoy could also make himself heard when calling for fly balls, although he couldn't hear the calls of his fellow fielders. Many historians also claim that Hoy was the reason that umpires adopted hand signals to go along with the vocal calls of "out," "safe" and "strike." This is not true, however. Hand signals were not used by umpires until 1905, three years after Hoy's playing career ended. At the age of 99, he threw out the ceremonial first pitch in Cincinnati prior to the third game of the 1961 World Series.

Cardinals

02
May

What is recognized as the first game in Cardinals history took place on this date in 1882. The Cards beat Louisville 9-7 before approximately 2,000 at Sportsman's Park, which was located on the west side of Grand at Dodier Street. A diamond had been laid out on the site as early as 1866, and major league baseball would be played there as late as 1966. Ballparks of the 1880s were primitive by today's standards, but Sportsman's Park was more luxurious than most. Permanent seating capacity was 6,000. The main grandstand had two decks from first base to third base. Later in 1886, bleachers were extended around the outfield fences and down the left and right field foul lines, increasing capacity to 12,000. The outfield distances were approximately 350 feet down the left field line, 460 feet to center, and 285 feet to right. The right field wall was actually a two-story house where Augustus Solari had been living. The Cardinals leased the land from him. After Solari vacated the residence, Chris Von Der Ahe turned it into a beer garden with handball courts and lawn bowling. The area was regarded as part of the playing field until October 1888, and right fielders often raced through the beer garden to chase down long drives. Another feature of the ballpark was a Japanese fireworks cannon made of bamboo and wrapped with steel wire.

Cardinals

03
May

Ted Breitenstein died on this date in 1935. Making his first major league start on October 4, 1891, Breitenstein pitched a no-hitter for the Cardinals, defeating Louisville 8-0 in the first game of a doubleheader at Sportsman's Park. The only man to reach base off Breitenstein was Harry Taylor, who drew a walk. Breitenstein also struck out six batters. Prior to the no-hitter Breitenstein made five relief appearances for the Cardinals totaling 19⅔ innings in which he was 1-0 with an ERA of 3.20. Louisville won the second contest, called after eight innings by darkness, 4-2. A native of St. Louis, Breitenstein was 22 when he made his big league debut and pitched for the Cardinals from 1891 through 1896 and again in 1901. He had a lifetime record of 160-170. Breitenstein pitched another no-hitter as a member of the Cincinnati Reds on April 22, 1898.

Cardinals

04
May

In the bottom of the tenth inning with the score 4-4 against the Reds on this date in 1901, a fire broke out at League Park in St. Louis. The fire was caused by a cigar or cigarette dropped into a pile of refuse beneath the stands at the foot of one of the main stairways. There was little alarm at first among the 6,000 in attendance as smoke curled up through the seats, and fans leisurely left the structure. The game was interrupted more from the curiosity of the players and the umpire than any sense of imminent danger. But the flames, fanned by a stiff breeze, spread rapidly, leading to a general panic. Many leapt to the ground from the grandstand, a distance of eight to ten feet, to escape the flames. When the firemen reached the park, the grandstand, pavilion and club offices were a mass of flames. By the time the fire was extinguished, most of the wooden structure was destroyed. Only the bleachers in deep center field were saved. In addition, a few streetcars sitting outside the park awaiting passengers for their return home caught fire. Some of the fencing of the racetrack across Natural Bridge Road was also burned. Fortunately, there were no reports of serious injuries.

Cardinals

05
May

On this date in 1901, the Reds defeated the Cardinals 7-5 before a crowd of 7,000 at Sportsman's Park. League Park was destroyed by fire on a Saturday afternoon, and with a large crowd expected on Sunday May 5, the Cards management didn't want to postpone the game. It was played at Sportsman's Park, three blocks away from League Park. Sportsman's Park was used by the Cardinals from 1881 through 1892 and had been converted into a facility for cycle races and other events. A diamond was laid out inside the oval of the race track, but the opening was too small for an adequate baseball field, and according to one newspaper report, the outfield "resembled a plowed field." Much of the crowd was placed behind ropes in the outfield. This setup turned the contest into a complete farce. According to the ground rules, balls hit into the crowd were doubles. The crowd was located just a dozen feet behind the outfielders, and routine fly balls landed in the crowd for two-base hits. There were 22 hits in the game, 13 of them doubles and two homers hit over the crowd.

Cardinals

06
May

On this date in 1917 the Cardinals defeated the Reds 4-0 and take over first place in the National League. True, they managed to hold the position for only one day, but for a franchise that had struggled throughout the early decades of the century, occupying first place, even for a day, was an accomplishment. The Cardinals ended up in third place that year, with an 82-70 record, one of the few winning records they posted in that era. In 1917, however, Branch Rickey had been hired as the team's general manager, and the organization began a slow turnaround that led to success in the 1920s. Quite rightly, Rickey is credited with that success, though the emergence of Rogers Hornsby as the best hitter in the league didn't hurt the team at all.

Cardinals

07
May

On this date in 1940, the Cardinals set club records with seven home runs and 49 total bases while drubbing the Brooklyn Dodgers 18-2. Johnny Mize and Eddie Lake each hit two homers, and Don Padgett, Stu Martin and Joe Medwick hit one each. The two home runs by Lake were the first two of his major league career. He would not hit another in 1940. Or 1941. Or '42. The next year, while playing for the Red Sox, he would hit his third homer. A diminutive middle infielder who was nicknamed *Sparky*, Lake hit a grand total of 39 home runs in 3,199 major league plate appearances. But on May 7, 1940, he obviously had eaten his Wheaties.

Cardinals

08
May

On this date in 1966, the Cardinals played their last game at the first Busch Stadium and lost 10-5 to the San Francisco Giants before 17,053. Willie Mays accounted for the last run at the ballpark with a homer in the eighth inning. On the final play, Alex Johnson bounced into a double play. In postgame ceremonies, August Busch presented a deed to the property to Richard Amberg, publisher of the *St. Louis Globe-Democrat* and president of the Herbert Hoover Boys Club. Stadium superintendent Bill Stocksick, who "planted" the original home plate in 1909, was given the honor of digging it up. He then carried the plate to a waiting helicopter, where it was taken downtown to the new Busch Memorial Stadium. Now known as the Herbert Hoover Boys and Girls Club, the organization still occupies the site. It serves 2,800 children, with 300 attending daily. A ball field is located in the northeast corner of the lot, near where left field was located at the original Busch Stadium.

Cardinals

09
May

On this date in 1949, third baseman Eddie Kazak hit a grand slam
in the eighth inning of a 14-5
win over the Dodgers in Brooklyn. It
was Kazak's first major league homer.
A 28-year-old rookie in 1949, Kazak
played well enough during the first half
of the season to make the All-Star team as
a starter. A native of the coal-mining region
of Pennsylvania, where he worked in the mines
alongside his father, it was remarkable that Kazak reached the majors at all. Born Edward Tzaczuk, he was wounded severely twice in
the European theater during World War II. He was first bayoneted
in the right arm in hand-to-hand fighting. Then, his right elbow was
crushed and three fingers were paralyzed by shrapnel and falling
mortar. He spent 18 months in recuperation and therapy in the
hospital. Surgeons advised Kazak to forget about playing baseball,
but he battled back. Shortly after the 1949 All-Star Game, however,
Kazak suffered an on-field injury that all but ended his career. A
chipped bone in his ankle shelved him for two months, and afterward, he was little more than a reserve and a pinch-hitter until his
career ended in 1952.

Cardinals

10
May

On this date in 1894, center fielder Frank Shugart became the first Cardinal to hit three homers in a game and the club smacked six homers for the first time in history, but St. Louis lost 18-9 to the Reds in Cincinnati. Tom Parrott gave up all six homers, though he helped himself with the bat by hitting a home run along with a double and two singles. The Reds scored 11 runs in the fifth inning off Pink Hawley. Heinie Peitz hit two homers for the Cardinals, and Doggie Miller clubbed one. Shugart, Peitz and Miller hit consecutive homers in the seventh inning. The back-to-back-to-back feat was another Cardinal first. Shugart also homered in the first and sixth innings. They were his first three homers of 1894. In 1892 and 1893 combined, he hit only one home run in 1,111 at-bats. The next Cardinal batter to hit three homers in a game was George Watkins in 1928. The Cards didn't hit six homers in a game again until 1940, and the club failed to hit three homers in a row once more until 1944.

Cardinals

11
May

At Baker Bowl in Philadelphia on this date in 1923, the Cardinals and Phillies combined for ten home runs and 79 total bases in a game won by the Phillies 20-14. Three of the ten homers belonged to Philadelphia's Cy Williams. The other home run hitters for the Phils were Johnny Mokan, who had two, and Frank Parkinson. For the Cardinals, Les Mann hit two and Eddie Dyer and losing pitcher Bill Sherdel one each. St. Louis had 22 hits in the game. The 79 total bases were a major league record for two teams in a game until the Reds and Rockies combined for 81 in a contest at Coors Field in 1999. There were 23 different Cardinals and Phillies players who collected hits in the contest, which is still a big league record. Eddie Dyer, who was normally a pitcher, started the game in left field and batted second in an eight-game experiment to try to turn him into an outfielder. Mann pinch-hit for Dyer and remained in the game, so the Cardinals got three homers out of their left fielders. The homer by Dyer was the second of two that he hit in 157 at-bats. The first came three days earlier at Baker Bowl.

Cardinals

12
May

On this date in 1966, the Cardinals opened Busch Memorial Stadium before 46,048 and won 4-3 in 12 innings over the Atlanta Braves on a 50-degree night. The first batter was Felipe Alou facing Ray Washburn, and he grounded out to second baseman Julian Javier. Later, Alou hit two home runs to give the Braves a 3-2 lead. Mike Shannon hit the first Cardinal homer in the ballpark. The Cardinals tied the score in the ninth on an RBI-single by Jerry Buchek. Lou Brock won the contest with a walk-off single. Don Dennis was the winning pitcher and Phil Niekro was the loser. Among those present were baseball commissioner William Eckert and NL president Warren Giles. A helicopter landed to deliver the American flag to open the game's festivities. The stadium wasn't quite complete, however. Gas to the concession stands wasn't hooked up and workers were still installing paneling in the elegant Stadium Club. Attendants had to ice the bottles of beer by hand because the refrigeration equipment wasn't working. The message board on the scoreboard and the mechanical rolling tarp weren't operating properly. The outfield was soggy and the infield still had patches of dirt. Those problems were corrected quickly. The Cardinals drew 1,712,980 fans in 1966, breaking the previous mark of 1,430,676 set in 1949.

Cardinals

13
May

On this date in 1958, Stan Musial collected his 3,000th career hit during a 5-3 win over the Cubs at Wrigley Field. Musial was left out of the starting line-up so that he could accomplish the historic feat in front of the hometown fans in St. Louis. However, with the Cubs leading 3-1 and a runner on base in the sixth inning, manager Fred Hutchinson called on Musial as a pinch hitter. Musial responded with a run-scoring double off Moe Drabowsky. The umpires halted the game to award the ball to Musial, who was lifted for a pinch-runner. The following day, Musial was honored in pregame ceremonies at Busch Stadium prior to a game against the Giants, and he dramatically smashed a home run in the first inning, sparking a 3-2 win. He entered the season needing 43 hits to reach number 3,000 and got them in a hurry with 46 hits in his first 92 at-bats at the age of 37. Musial finished the season with a .337 average and 17 homers.

Cardinals

14
May

On this date in 1938, the Cardinals won a thrilling 7-6 come-from-behind victory in 10 innings against the Reds at Sportsman's Park. Trailing 5-1 heading into the ninth, the Cardinals scored four runs to forge a tie. After Cincinnati plated a run in the top of the tenth, the Cardinals came back with two in the bottom half on a walk-off homer by Enos Slaughter for the win. In the end, the dramatic victory didn't count. The Reds filed a protest over a disputed hit by Cincinnati's Dusty Cooke. At Sportsman's Park, the roof projected over the playing field. In the sixth inning, Cooke hit a ball that struck the facing of the roof and bounced back onto the outfield grass. Cooke reached third base for a triple, but the Reds argued the call should have been a home run because if Cooke had hit the ball a few inches lower it would have missed the roof and settled into the grandstand for a home run. NL president Ford Frick ordered that the entire game be replayed. As a result of the incident, white markings were applied to the roof from the edge of the pavilion screen to center field, including two poles that supported the screen separating the pavilion seats from the center field bleachers. A new ground rule provided that any ball hitting any of the white marks and bouncing back on the field was a home run.

Cardinals

15
May

Today's trivia: When did the only all-St. Louis World Series take place?

The Browns resided in St. Louis from 1902 through 1953. The only American League pennant won by the franchise was in 1944 during World War II, which set the stage for a World Series between the Browns and the Cardinals. With both teams using Sportsman's Park as their home field, it was the third, and most recent World Series played entirely in one ballpark. The first two were in 1921 and 1922 when the Giants and Yankees met at the Polo Grounds. In compliance with an order from the Office of Defense Transportation to keep trains, planes and buses open for military personnel, tickets for the 1944 Fall Classic were sold only to individuals living in the St. Louis metropolitan area. The Browns won games one and three to take a two-games-to-one lead, but the Cardinals rebounded to take the next three to win the world championship. Newspapers of the day noted how quiet the crowds were during the Cardinals-Browns World Series. Fans seemed to have trouble knowing who to root for. In St. Louis, with two teams sharing one ballpark, fans weren't divided by neighborhood, as in Chicago.

Cardinals

16
May

On this date in 1916, Bill Doak out-dueled Grover Alexander to lead the Cardinals to a 1-0 win over the Phillies in St. Louis. Doak's career is largely forgotten now, but he was a consistently good pitcher in his day. He compiled a 144-136 record for the Cardinals from 1913 through 1924 and in 1929. He twice led the NL in ERA, and he pitched three one-hitters. His greatest contribution to baseball, however, was the invention of a baseball glove. In that era, fielders' mitts were little more than small leather pillows that protected the hand, but did little to aid in making a catch, particularly before being broken in. Players spent hours pounding in a satisfactory pocket, and some even cut out the palm of the glove to form a pocket. In 1919, Doak sketched a glove with a pocket already formed. He inserted a lace of leather strips between the thumb and the forefinger, which were previously connected with a single strip of leather. He took his sketches to the Rawlings Sporting Goods Company, and within a few years, the Doak glove was the most popular on the market. It protected the hand but also helped the fielder snag the ball. Fielding improved dramatically in the 1920s after the introduction of the mitt based on Doak's prototype. He continued to receive royalties from Rawlings, which earned him as much as $25,000 a year, until his death in 1954.

Cardinals

17
May

On this date in 1994, the Cardinals hurled a two-hit shutout in a 2-0 win over the Pirates at Three Rivers Stadium. The oddball aspect of the game was that they used six hurlers to do it, tying a National League record for most pitchers used in a shutout. Starter Tom Urbani pitched 7⅔ innings, allowing one hit. John Habyan relieved him and walked the only batter he faced. Then Rob Murphy, Mike Perez and Rich Rodriguez each pitched ⅓ of an inning, followed by Rene Arocha, who threw 1⅓ innings to close out the game. Urbani got the win, the second of his career.

18
May

Cardinals outfielder John Mabry hit for the cycle on this date in 1996. He also managed to do record the hits in sequential order: a single in the second inning, double in the third, triple in the fifth, and a home run in the seventh. Only 15 Cardinal players have hit for the cycle in the modern era. Ken Boyer did it twice. No doubt Mabry was thrilled to achieve this rare feat, but, unfortunately, the Colorado Rockies still managed to best the Redbirds on that day, scoring five runs in the ninth off Dennis Eckersley to pull out a 9-8 victory. Mabry also, if you will, signed for the cycle with the Cardinals during his 14-year career. He signed in 1991 after being selected by the team in the amateur draft. He left as a free agent after the 1998 season, but signed on again as a free agent in 2001. After one season he left again as a free agent but returned on a free agent signing in 2004. He was granted free agency after that season but, a month later, signed on one more time, completing a cycle of four contracts.

Cardinals

19 May

On this date in 1972, the Cardinals traded first baseman Joe Hague to the Reds for outfielder Bernie Carbo. It wasn't an especially memorable trade except that Carbo became the caretaker of a lucky charm—a stuffed gorilla named "Mighty Joe Young." It was given to him by its original owner, Cardinals pitcher Scipio Spinks, who was traded to the Cubs after the 1973 season. "Mighty Joe Young" wore a miniature Cardinals uniform and sat on the bench during games to bring luck to the team. The Cardinals finished with a losing record that year and managed only an 81-81 tally the following year, after which Carbo was dealt to the Red Sox. The change of scene apparently was helpful to Joe, who Carbo continued to bring to the dugout, though he didn't bother to change the gorilla's uniform. In 1975, as the Red Sox won the AL pennant, Joe enjoyed a bit of media attention, becoming the team's good-luck charm on their quest for the title, still wearing the Cards' uniform from his days in St. Louis.

Cardinals

20
May

The question of the day: Why did the Cardinals threaten to go on strike in 1947?

The Cardinals played a game against an African-American opponent for the first time since 1884 on May 6, 1947, and lost 7-6 to Jackie Robinson and the Dodgers in Brooklyn. Two days later, the AP issued a story that the Cardinals threatened to strike over the presence of Robinson on the Dodgers' roster. According to the report, the strike was averted by the intervention of NL president Ford Frick and Cards owner Sam Breadon. Frick publicly threatened to indefinitely suspend any player who refused to take the field with Robinson. The Cardinals "strike" remains a matter of controversy. Breadon and Cards manager Eddie Dyer denied the report. A number of Cardinals players insist to this day that there was never a strike threat. According to those on the club in 1947, there was grumbling about integration of the sport among Cardinals players, but no more than any other club including the Dodgers.

Cardinals

21
May

On this date, the birthday of Cleveland Indians star Earl Averill, we recall an unfortunate incident that derailed the career of Dizzy Dean, of the Cardinals' all-time great pitchers.

During the All-Star Game at Griffith Stadium in Washington on July 7, 1937, Dean broke his big toe when struck by a line drive off the bat of Averill, then with the Indians. Dean was the starting pitcher and slated to go three innings. He had one out remaining when struck by Averill's drive. The toe injury had serious consequences for Dean. Pitching just two weeks after the toe was broken, he came back much too soon. He was unable to push off the mound, which dramatically reduced the velocity of his pitches and put additional stress on his arm. Dean made seven starts after the All-Star break before being shut down during the last week of August. Only 27 when the injury occurred, Dean had a record of 133-72. After the 1937 All-Star break, he won only 17 more games.

Cardinals

22
May

The question of the day: Was Dean's career ruined by the toe injury or a sore arm?

Dean had been complaining of a sore arm in 1937 before breaking his toe, and there is little doubt that a brutal workload was an overriding factor in his decline. Dizzy's first professional season was in 1930 when he was 20 years old, and he pitched 311 innings in 47 games. In 1931, he went 304 innings in 14 games while still in the minors. Reaching the majors in 1932, Dean averaged 306 innings and 49 games (34 starts and 15 relief appearances) over five seasons through 1936. In addition to posting a 120-65 record from 1932 through 1936, he recorded 29 saves. He also pitched in exhibition games during the season as the Cardinals spent many off days playing in minor league towns to earn extra money. At the 1937 All-Star break, he had pitched 147⅔ innings, a pace that would have given him 339 innings by season's end. Given the number of innings and games he pitched at such a young age, it's amazing that Dean's arm didn't break down before 1937, and it's likely that an arm injury would have occurred even if Earl Averill's All-Star Game drive had missed his toe.

Cardinals

23
May

On this date in 1937, Dizzy Dean made a mockery of the balk rule during a 6-2 win over the Phillies at Sportsman's Park. Taking heed of National League president Ford Frick's ruling to come to a full stop between his wind-up and delivery, Dean came to a stop for a full three minutes before pitching to Jimmie Wilson with a runner on first in the second inning. On the next pitch, Dean stopped and stood still as a statue for four minutes before the umpires called a balk for holding up the game unnecessarily. Dean responded by sitting on the mound for another four minutes and was called for yet another balk for stalling. A few days later at a father-son luncheon in Belleview, Illinois, Dean called Frick and umpire George Barr "the two biggest crooks in baseball." Frick suspended Dean for three days for the remarks, but after a stormy meeting with Dizzy in New York, Frick reduced the suspension to two days with no loss of pay. Frick wanted Dean to sign a document retracting his remarks calling the NL president a "crook" but Dean refused.

Cardinals

24
May

Today's trivia: Which Cardinals legends have been honored by having their uniform numbers retired?

Players who have had their uniform numbers retired are Ozzie Smith (1), Red Schoendienst (2), Stan Musial (6), Enos Slaughter (9), Ken Boyer (14), Dizzy Dean (17), Lou Brock (20), Bruce Sutter (42) and Bob Gibson (45). The number 85 was retired in honor of August Busch on his 85th birthday. Number 51 hasn't been issued since Willie McGee played his last game in 1999. In addition, the Cardinals haven't given out number 57 since the death of Darryl Kile in 2002 or number 32 since the death of Josh Hancock in 2007. It's likely that Albert Pujols will be the last individual to don number 5 and Tony La Russa's number 10 will also certainly be retired at a future date.

Cardinals

25
May

Happy Birthday, Johnny Beazley, who was born on this date in 1918. As a rookie in 1942, Beazley had a 21-6 record and a 2.13 ERA, during the regular season. In the World Series, he was the winning pitcher in game one. Beazley took the mound in game five with the Cards leading three games to one, and clinched the title for St. Louis with a 4-2 complete game victory. Beazley spent the 1943, 1944 and 1945 seasons in the Army Air Corps, rising to the rank of captain. He spent much of his time in the South Pacific and pitched on service teams in between combat assignments. Beazley developed arm trouble in the military, however, because he was out of shape and didn't warm up properly before pitching an exhibition game staged for the benefit of the Army Relief Fund. Beazley tried to beg off the assignment because of the risk of injury due to his lack of physical conditioning, but his commanding officer ordered him to pitch. Beazley came back to the majors after the war ended, but pitched erratically with the Cards (1946) and Boston Braves (1947–49). His postwar record over those four seasons was 9-6 with a 4.39 ERA in 149⅔ innings.

Cardinals

26
May

The question of the day: When did future Hall of Famers John McGraw and Wilbert Robinson sign contracts to play for the Cardinals?

John McGraw and Wilbert Robinson signed to play for the Cardinals on May 8, 1900. They were purchased from the defunct Baltimore Orioles on February 11, but refused to sign with the Cards for nearly three months. Both agreed only after the club struck the reserve clause from their contracts, making them free agents at the end of the season, an unheard-of concession. When McGraw and Robinson arrived in St. Louis, Cardinals' management arranged to have them met at the train station by a brass band. McGraw was one of the top third basemen in baseball at the time, and Robinson ranked among the elite catchers, but the Cardinals should have passed on both. McGraw hit .344 with an on-base percentage of .517, but was limited to 99 games because he missed two lengthy stretches. He was spiked during a play in June and was out with boils in August. To make room for McGraw, the Cardinals sold third baseman Lave Cross to the Dodgers. Cross was 34, but still had five solid seasons ahead of him.

Cardinals

27
May

The question of the day: What happened when John McGraw and Wilbert Robinson played their first game with the Cardinals?

The arrival of John McGraw and Wilbert Robinson brought a clamor for tickets, but a streetcar strike made it difficult to reach the ballpark. Between 6,000 and 7,000 attended the game, well above the average that season. According to newspaper reports, "The crush of wagons around the park made a sight long to be remembered." There was gridlock for blocks in every direction. It was estimated that 1,500 wagons and 2,000 horses were crowded around the park and the confusion was "beyond description." Amid the traffic crush were a few of the first automobiles to traverse the streets of St. Louis. McGraw and Robinson were presented with a gold cane, silk umbrella, and several floral horseshoes. McGraw made an error that contributed to three Dodger runs in the ninth inning, and the Cardinals lost 5-4. At the end of the season, McGraw and Robinson signed with the newly formed Baltimore Orioles of the American League. On their way out of St. Louis while crossing the Eads Bridge, the pair tossed their uniforms out of the train window and into the Mississippi River.

Cardinals

28
May

On this date in 1949, Cardinals owner Fred Saigh announced plans for a new stadium. Plans called for a 47,000-seat stadium built for $4 million. Plans drawn by architect Syl G. Schmidt had a horseshoe-shaped grandstand in three tiers and uncovered bleachers in the outfield. The design was somewhat similar to that of Memorial Stadium in Baltimore, which served as the home of the Orioles from 1954 through 1991, but with a cleaner more modern approach, much like Dodger Stadium, which opened in 1962. Saigh refused to disclose the location of the new ballpark but said it would be built on 18 acres he owned and that he hoped to acquire eight or nine more acres. At the time, only two ballparks in the majors had been built since 1915. Those were Yankee Stadium, constructed in 1923, and Municipal Stadium in Cleveland, opened in 1932. Saigh's stadium never got past the planning stages, however.

Cardinals

29
May

A bizarre play in which Ozzie Smith singled into a double play highlighted a 4-2 loss to the Padres at Busch Memorial Stadium on this date in 1982. Joaquin Andujar set the stage by lining a single to center. Smith followed with a single to right. Andujar rounded second but stopped in his tracks when San Diego right fielder Sixto Lezcano's throw came in behind him. After a brief rundown, third baseman Luis Salazar tagged out Andujar, who then jarred the ball from Salazar's glove. Padres shortstop Garry Templeton, uncertain whether Andujar had been retired, swiped at the loose ball and scooped it toward third base. However, no one was covering the bag and Smith charged toward second and rounded the base with a notion of heading to third. Left fielder Alan Wiggins retrieved the ball and threw to Templeton, who tagged out Smith before he could retreat to second.

30
May

The morning game of a Memorial Day doubleheader between the Cardinals and Senators in Washington was postponed on this date in 1898 when a railroad bridge washed out, which delayed the Cardinals train from St. Louis. To make the afternoon contest, the Baltimore and Ohio train traveled the 152 miles from Cumberland, Maryland, to Washington in three hours and five minutes, which at the time was a speed record. Oddly, Cards manager Tim Hurst wasn't on the train. He disembarked at the station in East St. Louis to eat a frankfurter only to watch the train pull away without him. Hurst took another locomotive to Washington. After finally arriving in the nation's capital, the Cardinals lost to the Senators 5-3.

Cardinals

31
May

The question of the day: During the period from 1902 through 1953 when St. Louis fielded two major league teams, who won the attendance war?

In the early years, the fight for the box office was about even. The Browns drew more fans than the Cardinals in 1902, 1903, from 1905 through 1908, in 1918 and 1919, and each season from 1922 through 1925. The Cardinals won nine NL pennants from 1926 through 1946, while the Browns were usually at or near the bottom of the AL standings. The disparity in success gave the Cards a firm advantage in attendance. The highest season attendance figure for the Browns during the 1930s was 179,126 in 1932. The club bottomed out at just 80,922 in 1935. The Browns outdrew the Cards only once from 1926 through 1953. That was in 1944 when both clubs won pennants. The Browns attracted 508,644 that season, a jump from 214,392 in 1943. The Cards fell from 517,135 in 1943 to 461,968 in 1944. By the end of the decade, the Cardinals had reestablished themselves as the dominant franchise in St. Louis. In 1949, the Cardinals outdrew the Browns 1,430,767 to 270,936, a margin of more than 5-to-1.

Cardinals

June

Cardinals

01
June

Milt Thompson's bizarre broken-bat single in the tenth inning on this date in 1991 ended a 6-5 win over the Mets at Busch Stadium. With the score 5-5 and Cardinal Gerald Perry on third base, Thompson's bat shattered when he made contact with a John Franco pitch. The ball and half of Thompson's bat whizzed toward first baseman Dave Magadan at the same time. Magadan had to make a split-second decision. If he fielded the ball, he risked serious injury from being struck by the flying bat. If he ducked out of the way, Thompson's hit would win the game for the Cardinals. Magadan chose to duck, and Perry crossed the plate with the winning run.

Cardinals

02
June

The question of the day: How did a B-17 bomber interrupt the first game of the 1943 World Series between the Yankees and the Cardinals on October 5?

In the eighth inning, a B-17 zoomed low over Yankee Stadium, startling the crowd of 68,676. It swung back two minutes later and returned again five minutes after the second pass. This third pass was frightening, as the huge four-engine bomber was no more than 200 feet off the ground and hedge-hopped the roof, narrowly missing the flagpoles. The roar of the plane drowned out the nationwide radio broadcast and stopped play as players stood and watched the aircraft. New York Mayor Fiorello LaGuardia was furious and demanded that the Army Air Force discipline the pilot. Second Lieutenant Jack Watson was fined $75 and confined to barracks for a few days for the indiscretion before being sent to England with his plane on October 10. On January 11, 1944, Watson's plane was badly shot up during a mission over Germany. He landed his burning plane in England, but not before his crew of eight bailed out. Four landed in the water and drowned, three were taken as POWs, and one evaded capture. In all, Watson completed 35 combat missions in 1943 and 1944.

03
June

On this date in 1918, the Cardinals won a weird 12-inning, 15-12 decision over the Dodgers at Ebbets Field. In the first inning, the Cards scored two runs before the Dodgers countered with six in their half. St. Louis responded with seven runs in the sixth inning for a 9-6 lead after only an inning-and-a-half had been played. Brooklyn took an 11-9 advantage in the fourth. The Redbirds surged ahead again 12-11 in the eighth, only to have Brooklyn score in the ninth to tie the contest. The issue was settled with three Cardinals runs in the 12th. The Cards were helped by umpire Cy Rigler. In the sixth inning, with Doug Baird of the Cardinals as a base runner on second, Watson Cruise knocked a low liner to center, which Dodger outfielder Dave Hickman held momentarily, then dropped. Baird reached third and, believing the ball was caught, started back for second. After going about 20 feet, Baird realized that Hickman had failed to hold onto Cruise's drive. Instead of touching third again, Baird cut across the diamond and scored. Rigler counted the run despite the protests of the Dodgers. According to Rigler, Baird had legally touched third base, and didn't need to do so again. At the time, there was nothing in the rulebook specifically addressing the situation.

Cardinals

04
June

On this date in 1918, umpire Cy Rigler was a source of controversy for the second day in a row. The Cardinals scored seven runs in the 13th against the Dodgers in Brooklyn with help from a disputed grand slam by Marty Kavanaugh. With the score 1-1, Kavanaugh drove the ball down the third base line. Rigler ruled it fair, but the Dodgers made no attempt to field the ball, claiming it was foul. During the course of the argument, Kavanaugh rounded the bases for the grand slam. Dozens of fans rushed onto the field to get at Rigler. Players prevented them from reaching the umpire, with the exception of one individual who punched Rigler in the neck.

Cardinals

05
June

Today's trivia: How did the Cardinals blow a chance at the World Series in 1996?

In Tony La Russa's first year as manager, the Cardinals had a record of 88-74 in 1996 and swept the Padres in the Division Series. The opponent in the NLCS was the Atlanta Braves, a club that finished 96-66 and were the defending world champions, having beaten the Indians in six games in the 1995 World Series. During the regular season, the Cards were 4-9 against Atlanta and lost all six games at Busch Stadium. The Cardinals lost the first game against the Braves, but then won three in a row. In game four at Busch Stadium, St. Louis trailed 3-0 before scoring three runs in the seventh and one in the eighth, on a home run by Brian Jordan, to win 4-3. But the Cardinals were outscored 32-1 over the last three games of the series, losing 14-0, 3-1 and 15-0. The Braves won the first two games of the World Series against the Yankees 12-1 and 4-0 in New York to compile a five-game postseason winning streak in which they outscored the opposition 48-2. But the Yankees came back to win four in a row to win the championship. The Yankee manager was Joe Torre, who managed the Cardinals from August 1990 through June 1995.

Cardinals

06
June

On this date in 1948, Red Schoendienst led the attack as the Cardinals swept the Phillies 11-1 and 2-0 during an eventful doubleheader in St. Louis. He collected three doubles and a homer in the opener. Combined with his three doubles the day before, Schoendienst tied a major league record for most extra base hits in consecutive games (seven) and another for most doubles in back-to-back games (six). He tied a Cardinals record for most extra base hits in a game (four). Schoendienst continued his hot streak in the second game with a pair of doubles. This tied a major league mark for most extra base hits in a doubleheader (six) and a National League record for most doubles in a doubleheader (five). Over three consecutive games, Schoendienst had eight doubles and a home run. The Cardinals also set a team record for most homers in an inning with four in the sixth inning of the opener. In a span of six batters, Erv Dusak, Schoendienst, Enos Slaughter and Nippy Jones all went deep off Phillies pitcher Charles Bicknell. It is the only time in Cardinals history that the club hit four homers in an inning.

Cardinals

07
June

Today's trivia: Who was Patsy Tebeau?

Born in 1864, Patsy Tebeau was the manager of the Cleveland Spiders from 1891 through 1898 and the Cardinals in 1899 and 1900. A native of the gang-infested section of St. Louis known as Goose Hill, Tebeau was known as a tough, aggressive leader who fought for every advantage and insisted that his players did the same. Although none of his clubs won a pennant, they usually led the league in fights. Tebeau's outfits baited umpires, spiked opponents, beaned batters, and circumvented the rules with regularity. The contemporary press often referred to the Spiders and Cardinals as "hooligans." After he was fired by the Cardinals in August 1900 when he was only 35, Tebeau never returned to baseball. While operating a saloon in St. Louis in 1918, Tebeau committed suicide, shooting himself with a revolver that he tied to his right wrist.

Cardinals

08
June

Cardinals manager Patsy Tebeau, Phillies skipper Bill Shettsline and umpire Oyster Burns had a disagreement over the playing conditions during a game in Philadelphia on this date in 1899. The Cards scored three times in the top of the sixth inning to take a 4-3 lead as it began to rain steadily. Shettsline wanted Burns to call the game, and Tebeau ridiculed Shettsline by calling him a "quitter." The Phillies responded with five tallies in their half to take an 8-4 advantage, and Burns called the contest because of the driving rain. Tebeau objected and followed Burns under the grandstand looking for a fight. Burns called for a policeman, who threatened to put Tebeau out into the street in full uniform in the midst of a throng of Philadelphia fans. Tebeau promised to be "good" and was allowed to sit on the bench while Burns left the ballpark safely.

09
June

On this date in 1950, Baseball Commissioner Happy Chandler informed Cardinals owner Fred Saigh that he couldn't schedule a game on a Sunday. The Sunday night dispute originated with the postponement of a night game between the Dodgers and Cardinals in St. Louis on June 3. The next day, Saigh announced that Dodger president Branch Rickey agreed to replay the contest on Sunday night July 16 as part of a day-night doubleheader. Chandler told Saigh that Major League Baseball rules prohibited the playing of games on Sunday nights. The game was rescheduled for Monday July 17. The dispute between Saigh and Chandler would have long-lasting consequences. Chandler's contract as commissioner expired in April 1952. Saigh began a one-man campaign to oust Chandler and lined up enough fellow owners to prevent an extension of Chandler's contract when it came up for a vote in December 1950. Chandler resigned in September 1951. The first Sunday night game in major league history took place in June 1963 in Houston.

Cardinals

10
June

On this date in 1944, the Cardinals faced a 15-year-old pitcher during an 18-0 win over the Reds in Cincinnati. The Cards came into the contest with just one run in their previous 25 innings. The 18-0 decision set a club record for most runs in a shutout. The carnage could have been worse. The Cardinals tied a National League record for most runners left on base in a nine-inning game with 18. Reds pitchers gave up 21 hits and 14 walks. The last five runs were scored in the ninth inning off Cincinnati pitcher Joe Nuxhall, who was making his major league debut at the age of 15, thereby becoming the youngest player in modern major league history. Many teams employed teenagers at the time because of the World War II manpower shortage, but none was as young as Nuxhall. He didn't pitch in his second major league game until 1952, but had a playing career that lasted until 1966. Afterward, he became the Reds radio broadcaster, a job he held until his death in 2007.

Cardinals

11 June

Today's trivia: Who did the Cardinals trade to acquire Mark McGwire?

The Cardinals traded T. J. Mathews, Eric Ludwick and Blake Stein to the Athletics on July 31, 1997, for Mark McGwire. The impact of the acquisition of McGwire for three undistinguished players cannot be understated. When he came to St. Louis, McGwire was 33 years old and had 363 career homers. He first gained national attention in 1987 when he set the all-time major league record for home runs by a rookie with 49 for the A's. The previous record was 36. It would be nine years before McGwire reached that home run figure again as he battled injuries and prolonged slumps. His nadir was 1991, when he batted .201 with 22 home runs in 154 games. McGwire seemed to be back on track in 1996 with a .312 average and 52 home runs. He had hit 34 homers for Oakland in 1997 when they dealt him to the Cardinals. McGwire came cheaply because his contract was due to expire at the end of the season and the A's had almost no hope of signing him. Oakland had a record of 42-68 and was out of postseason contention. The trade reunited McGwire with Tony La Russa, who managed him from the start of his career through 1995.

Cardinals

12
June

Today's trivia: Why was the McGwire trade a gamble for the Cardinals?

The Cardinals had no guarantee that McGwire would help them reach the playoffs in 1997 (they were seven games out of first) or that he would return to St. Louis in 1998. He was a native Californian and was known to favor going to a West Coast team. To the surprise of many, he inked a three-year deal, with an option for a fourth, which kept him in St. Louis. McGwire loved the family atmosphere, enthusiasm and baseball tradition in St. Louis, and he had a strong relationship with La Russa. The Cardinals reaped the benefits of the deal in 1998 when McGwire mania swept the nation as he chased Roger Maris's single-season home run record. McGwire's remarkable 70-home run season brought a huge amount of attention to St. Louis and packed the stadium night after night. His affection for the city and his high-profile charity work made McGwire a bona fide civic hero. He followed his record-breaking season with 65 more homers in 1999. In 1,739 at-bats with the Cardinals before his retirement in 2001, McGwire hit 220 home runs.

Cardinals

13
June

Von McDaniel, an 18-year-old Cardinals pitcher only weeks out of high school, made his major league debut on this date in 1957 with four innings of relief during a 5-1 loss to the Phillies in Philadelphia. A native of Hollis, Oklahoma, he was signed by the Cardinals on May 27 for $50,000. His brother Lindy, who was three years older, was also signed by the Cards for $50,000 in 1955. At the time, major league rules stipulated that any player who signed a contract for more than $4,000 out of high school or college must spend two years on the major league roster. Three days after his debut, Von again pitched four innings of relief, and allowed no runs and a hit. He made his first major league start on June 21, 1957, and pitched a two-hit shutout to defeat the Dodgers 2-0 in St. Louis. In his third start, on July 2, he retired the first 18 Milwaukee Braves batters to face him before surrendering two runs and five hits in 7⅔ innings. On July 28, he hurled a one-hitter against the Pirates in St. Louis, and retired the last 22 batters. At 18 years and 91 days, he became the youngest pitcher in modern major league history to pitch a no-hitter or a one-hitter. With his spectacular debut, Von became a tremendous gate attraction. His final stats in 1957 included a 7-5 record and a 3.22 ERA.

Cardinals

14
June

The question of the day: What happened to the McDaniel brothers after 1957?

Von McDaniel pitched only two games and two major league innings after 1957 in which he posted an earned run average of 13.50. He suffered a severely torn shoulder muscle during spring training in 1958, and his big league career was over at 19. He moved to third base and played in the minors as late as 1966, but he never hit well enough to make it back to the majors. Von's brother Lindy also struggled in 1958, but became a relief pitcher in 1959. Lindy played for the Cardinals until 1962 and in the majors until 1975. Although he never played in the postseason during his 21-year major league career, he appeared in 987 big league games, which at the time was second in history to Hoyt Wilhelm. During the magical summer of 1957, St. Louis newspapers reported on the exploits of 13-year-old Kerry Don McDaniel in amateur games in Hollis. In 1962, Kerry Don became the third McDaniel brother to sign with the Cardinals for $50,000. Unlike his brothers, Kerry Don began his professional career in the minors and never reached the big leagues.

Cardinals

15
June

Rookie pitcher Dizzy Dean jumped the club in a salary dispute on this date in 1932. Dean had been threatening to quit for weeks, claiming mistreatment from Cardinals management, which repeatedly denied Dean's demands for a pay boost. Dean claimed his contract should be voided because he was underage when he signed it and petitioned commissioner Kenesaw Landis to declare him a free agent. After an investigation by Landis revealed that Dean was 21 when he signed the document, the commissioner denied the request and Dean returned to the club two days later. Only 22, he was 18-15 with an ERA of 3.30 in 1932. He led the NL in innings pitched (286), strikeouts (191) and shutouts (four). The son of a poor Arkansas sharecropper, Dean was an immediate fan favorite with his winning personality. His pitching alone would have been enough to immortalize him, but his bold and zany antics on and off the field made him one of the most recognizable figures in America. A relentless braggart who had a burning need to be the center of attention and who overreacted to the slightest affront, Dean relied on his field performance and tremendous drawing power to get away with his eccentricities and his almost constant battles with club management.

Cardinals

16
June

On this date in 1996, the Cardinals fired Joe Torre as manager and hired Mike Jorgensen to replace him. Torre was dismissed while the Cardinals held a record of 20-27. He was 351-354 as manager of the Cards from 1990 through 1995. It was the third time that Torre was fired as manager. His previous stints were with the Mets (1977–81) and Braves (1982–84). At the time the Cardinals canned him, Torre's career record in 14 seasons as manager was 894-1,003. At that point he had never managed a team in the World Series, nor had he appeared in one in 18 seasons as a player (1960–77). The Yankees saw something in Torre, however, and hired him as manager on November 2, 1995. In his first season in pinstripes, Torre managed the Yanks to a world championship, the first for the franchise since 1978. It was the start of one of the most successful runs in big league history. Torre also managed the Yankees to the world championship in 1998, 1999 and 2000 and to World Series appearances in 2001 and 2003. On October 23, 1995, the Cards replaced Jorgensen with Tony La Russa.

Cardinals

17
June

The question of the day: When did the Cardinals overcome an 11-run deficit to win a game?

Trailing 11-0, the Cardinals made an amazing comeback to win 14-12 over the Giants in the first game of a doubleheader at the Polo Grounds on June 15, 1952. The Giants took the lead with five runs in the second inning and six in the third. Believing the game was in the bag, New York manager Leo Durocher removed two of his regulars to rest them for the second game of the twinbill. Cards manager Eddie Stanky contemplated the same strategy before St. Louis struck back with seven runs in the fifth, three in the seventh and two in the eighth to take a 12-11 lead. Cards shortstop Solly Hemus tied the score with a homer. Enos Slaughter broke the deadlock with a single. The Redbirds added two insurance tallies in the ninth before the Giants added one more. The rally set a National League record (since tied) for the largest deficit overcome to win a game. The Cards failed to score the rest of the day. New York won the second game 3-0 in a contest called after seven innings by darkness. At the time, NL rules prevented lights from being used to finish games played on a Sunday.

Cardinals

18
June

On this date in 1940, just six days after being traded from the Cardinals to the Dodgers, Joe Medwick was beaned by St. Louis pitcher Bob Bowman in the first inning of an 11-inning, 7-5 victory over Brooklyn at Ebbets Field. Bowman denied throwing intentionally at Medwick, but few believed him. Bowman had exchanged words with Medwick and Dodgers manager Leo Durocher that morning at Manhattan's Hotel New Yorker. According to Durocher, Bowman shouted, "I'll take care of both of you guys! Wait and see!" On Medwick's first at-bat, he was hit in the temple with a fastball, which gave him a severe concussion. The next day, Durocher sought out Bowman at the hotel, and the two nearly came to blows. National League president Ford Frick spent several days accumulating testimony from nearly everyone on both clubs but absolved Bowman of any blame. Medwick was playing again in four days. With tensions still high the day after Medwick's beaning, Cardinals catcher Mickey Owen took exception to a remark by Durocher and charged the Brooklyn dugout in the third inning of an 8-3 St. Louis defeat. Players from both teams joined in the melee, which was broken up by the umpires. Owen was fined $50 by Frick for "conduct tending to incite disorder."

Cardinals

19
June

On this date in 1918, five Cardinals and the wife of one of the players narrowly escaped death or serious injury in an accident north of Buffalo, New York. The Cards were traveling from Boston to St. Louis, a trip that required a four-hour layover in Buffalo for a change in trains. Bill Doak, Jakie May, Walton Cruise, Cliff Heathcote, Doug Baird and Baird's wife decided to take advantage of the delay by taking a quick jaunt to Niagara Falls. The group rented a car, but 15 miles out of Buffalo a tire blew out, causing the auto to turn over. The top was down and the six were thrown clear, escaping with only scrapes and bruises. Mrs. Baird was drenched in gasoline, which fortunately did not ignite.

Cardinals

20
June

The question of the day: Why did the Cardinals forfeit a game in 1954?

On July 18, 1954, the temperature in St. Louis reached 112 degrees, and the Cardinals played a contentious doubleheader against the Phillies at Busch Stadium. Rain caused a delay of more than an hour in the first game, which went ten innings before the Phillies won 11-10. As a result, the second contest didn't start until 6:48. In the fifth inning, with the Phillies leading 8-1 and darkness setting in, Cards manager Eddie Stanky began stalling because he mistakenly believed that lights couldn't be turned on to complete a Sunday contest. That was true before 1954, but the rule was changed just before the start of the season. Stanky changed pitchers twice during the inning, and his hurlers spent as much time as possible between pitches, which were nowhere near the plate. When Stanky called for a third reliever, Pirelli forfeited the game to the Phillies. The decision drew a derisive cheer from St. Louis fans. NL president Warren Giles suspended Stanky for five days and fined him $100.

Cardinals

**21
June**

The question of the day: What two players fought before the second game of the July 18, 1954 twinbill was called by forfeit?

Just prior to umpire Babe Pirelli's decision to end the game, Cards catcher Al Years and Phillies first baseman Earl Torgeson fought They began exchanging words after Torgeson was nearly hit by a pitch, which touched off a melee in which players from both sides swarmed the field and began swinging and punching indiscriminately. Phillies manager Terry Moore, a long-time Cardinals star outfielder during the 1940s whom Eddie Stanky fired as coach two years earlier, grabbed Years. Stanky, in turn, sent Moore to the ground with an old-fashioned football tackle. Both Stanky and Moore sported facial injuries after the skirmish. The extreme heat created another unusual situation. In the first game, catchers Stan Lopata of the Phillies and Bill Sarna of the Cards discarded their chest protectors believing the risk of being hit in the shoulder, ribs or abdomen outweighed being bogged down by extra equipment on the torrid day.

Cardinals

22
June

The Cardinals purchased Grover Alexander from the Cubs on this date in 1926. Alexander was 39 years old but had a 318-171 lifetime record when acquired by the Cardinals. He was 3-3 in 1926 when purchased from the Cubs. Chicago wanted to get rid of Alexander because he constantly feuded and defied the authority of new manager Joe McCarthy. Alexander showed up drunk six of his last ten days with the club and twice failed to show up for a game. During one contest, he collapsed on the bench in a drunken stupor. The Cards picked up Alexander at the urging of coach Bill Killefer, who was a teammate of the pitcher with the Phillies and Cubs and was manager of the Cubs from 1921 through 1925. Killefer had long been a steadying influence on Alexander, who helped the Cardinals win two pennants and a world championship. He was 9-7 over the remainder of the 1926 season, won game six of the World Series, and earned a dramatic save in the game seven clincher. In 1927, Alexander was 21-10 and posted a 16-9 mark in 1928 before age caught up with him.

Cardinals

23 June

Willie McGee had a career day on this date in 1984 by hitting for the cycle and driving in six runs during a game televised nationally by NBC-TV, but he was upstaged by Ryne Sandberg as the Cardinals lost 12-11 to the Cubs in 11 innings at Wrigley Field. The Cards led 9-3 in the sixth but allowed Chicago back in the game. With the score 9-8 and two outs in the ninth, Sandberg homered off Bruce Sutter to send the contest into extra innings. McGee completed the cycle in the tenth with an RBI-double off Lee Smith. McGee scored on David Green's single to give the Redbirds an 11-9 advantage. Sandberg stepped to the plate again in the bottom half and hit a two-run homer off Sutter to tie the tilt again 11-11. The Cubs won it in the 11th on a walk-off pinch-single by Dave Owen. The first three hits in McGee's cycle were a bases-loaded triple against Steve Trout in the second inning, a single off Rick Bordi in the fourth and a homer versus Dickie Noles in the sixth.

Cardinals

24
June

On this date in 1900, Cardinal outfielder Mike Donlin was stabbed during an altercation outside of a St. Louis saloon at 4:00 a.m. Donlin and teammate Gus Weyhing were carousing on Washington Avenue near Eleventh Street. Donlin began teasing a man about his large red beard when the man's companion took offense and tore at Donlin with a knife. Donlin was stabbed several times in the cheek and in the neck, just missing the jugular vein. He grabbed at the knife and his fingers were cut badly. The assailant took off and was never apprehended. At the hospital, Donlin hoped to avoid publicity by giving his occupation as "machinist," but he was recognized and the story hit the papers. Donlin missed nearly two months from his injuries. He played for the Cardinals in 1899 and 1900. He compiled a lifetime batting average of .333 in 1,050 games between 1899 and 1914 and might have been one of the greatest stars in the history of the game if he had taken the sport more seriously and controlled his personal life. In 1902 with the Orioles, he was sentenced to six months in jail for assaulting an actress and her escort. He missed the entire 1907 season in a salary dispute with the Giants and after batting .334 in 1908, sat out the 1909 and 1910 seasons to tour the vaudeville circuit in a successful act with his wife, an actress named Mabel Hite.

Cardinals

**25
June**

On this date in 1999, rookie pitcher Jose Jiminez recorded a no-hitter to beat Randy Johnson and the Diamondbacks 1-0 in Phoenix. The no-hitter was completely unexpected. In his 11 starts prior to the no-hitter, Jiminez had a record of 1-7 and an ERA of 8.04 in 59⅔ innings. He was the first Cardinal to pitch a no-hitter since Bob Forsch in 1983. The lone run of the game scored in the top of the ninth on an RBI-double by Thomas Howard off Johnson, who struck out 14 during the evening. Right fielder Eric Davis saved the no-hitter with two diving catches, including a one-out grab in the ninth of a sinking liner off the bat of David Delucci. Jiminez then retired Tony Womack for the final out on a slow roller to Joe McEwing at second base. Jiminez walked two, struck out eight, faced only 28 batters, and made 101 pitches. On June 30, in his first start after the no-hitter, Jiminez was tagged for seven runs in 4⅔ innings against the Astros in Houston. But in his second start following the no-hitter, Jiminez spun a two-hitter and defeated Johnson and the Diamondbacks 1-0 again, this time in St. Louis. Those proved to be the only two complete games of his career. He was 5-14 with a 5.85 ERA in 1999 and was dealt to the Rockies in November. Jiminez finished his career in 2004 with a 24-44 record and a 4.92 ERA.

26
June

On this date in 1934, a scene was filmed for the movie *Death on the Diamond* before a 13-7 win over the Dodgers at Sportsman's Park. The scene started with two Cardinals on base and Ernie Orsatti at bat. Orsatti slammed a lone drive into left-center where it was kicked around by the fielder, who threw wildly past third. Sprinting toward the plate, Orsatti suddenly collapsed in a heap. The Brooklyn catcher rushed out, retrieved the ball, and tagged Orsatti. Umpire Bill Klem made the "out" call with a big sweeping gesture. The Cardinals rushed from the dugout and surrounded their fallen teammate. *Death on the Diamond*, starring Robert Young, was released in September. In the story, Cardinals players were being murdered one by one. Young played a rookie pitcher who solved the mystery. He is best known for his roles on the television series *Father Knows Best* (1954–63) and *Marcus Welby M.D.* (1969–76). Orsatti also acted and was a stuntman in Hollywood films, including those of Buster Keaton. Orsatti later became an agent. Two of his sons became well-known stunt men in both movies and television.

Cardinals

27
June

Today's trivia: When did the Cardinals steal four bases on one pitch?

The Cardinals stole four bases on one pitch during a 14-inning, 9-8 loss to the Cubs at Wrigley Field on August 1, 1985. In the third inning, rookie left fielder Vince Coleman dove head-first into third base after Willie McGee swiped second. Coleman over-slid the bag, however, and after regaining his feet, realized he couldn't get back to third base and headed home. Third baseman Ron Cey threw to catcher Jody Davis, who ran Coleman back toward third and threw to Cey. Coleman reversed field, ran past Davis, and because pitcher Scott Sanderson was covering third instead of home, scored easily. Meanwhile, McGee went to third. Both Coleman and McGee were credited with two stolen bases on the play. Prior to Coleman's arrival, the major league record for stolen bases by a rookie was 73. Coleman, who ran a 9.4 100-yard dash while at Florida A&M, shattered that mark with 110 steals in 1985 while winning the Rookie of the Year Award. In addition to leading the league in stolen bases, Coleman hit .267 and scored 107 runs.

Cardinals

28
June

The question of the day: Where did Vince Coleman play at the start of the 1985 season?

Coleman started the season at the Cardinals' Class AAA affiliate in Louisville but was called up after an injury sidelined Tito Landrum. Coleman was expected to stay on the roster only until Landrum recovered, but he never went back to the minors. In his first game, on April 18, Coleman was 1-for-3 with two stolen bases. In his second game, the following day, he had four hits, including a double and a triple, and drove in the winning run as the Cardinals defeated the Pirates 5-4 at Busch Stadium. His 110 steals in 1985 have been topped in modern times only by Rickey Henderson (130 in 1982) and Lou Brock (118 in 1974). Coleman didn't stop there. He swiped 107 bases in 1986 and 109 in 1987 to record three of the six highest single-season stolen base marks since 1900. Coleman is also the only player in modern times to steal at least 100 bases three years in a row. He led the NL in steals six seasons in succession (1985-90). Coleman played on the Florida A&M football team as a punter. His cousin, Greg Coleman, who also matriculated at the school, was a punter in the NFL for six seasons.

Cardinals

29
June

Happy Birthday, Burgess White-head. Born on this date in 1910, Cardinals infielder Whitehead was the innocent victim of the circus atmosphere in Cincinnati in a game won 6-2 by the Cardinals over the Reds on June 6, 1933. The chaotic day began with Dizzy Dean fighting Reds pitcher Paul Derringer in front of the grandstand during batting practice. Dazzy Vance of the Cardinals stepped between them and broke up the Dizzy-Derringer duel. During the game, St. Louis outfielder George Watkins and Reds manager Jewel Ens were ejected for arguing too strenuously with the umpiring crew. In the ninth inning, Reds outfielder Harry Rice was knocked silly from a collision with the outfield wall while chasing a drive off the bat of Joe Medwick, who circled the bases for an inside-the-park home run. Finally, Whitehead leaned out of the dugout and was conked on the shoulder by a bottle thrown by a woman from the second deck.

Cardinals

30
June

Making his major league debut on this date in 1954, Joe Cunningham of the Cardinals hit a three-run homer in the fifth inning and a two-run single in the ninth during an 11-3 win over the Reds in Cincinnati. In his second game a day later, Cunningham clouted two homers and drove in four runs in a 9-2 victory over the Braves in Milwaukee. Both homers came off Warren Spahn. After two big league games, Cunningham had three homers and nine RBI. He is the only player in modern times to hit three homers in his first two games in the majors. Cunningham played for the Cardinals until 1961 and in the majors until 1966, but he was never a consistent home run threat. As a Cardinal, Cunningham hit 52 homers in 2,183 at-bats, but batted an impressive .304. Among Cardinals with at least 2,000 plate appearances with the club, Cunningham's .413 on-base percentage ranks sixth behind Mark McGwire, Albert Pujols, Rogers Hornsby, Stan Musial and Johnny Mize. After his playing days ended, Cunningham worked in the Cardinals front office in the speakers bureau and promotions department.

July

Cardinals

01
July

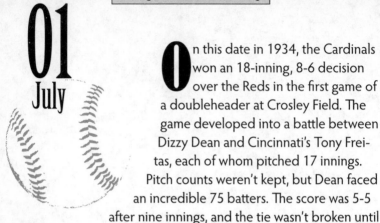

On this date in 1934, the Cardinals won an 18-inning, 8-6 decision over the Reds in the first game of a doubleheader at Crosley Field. The game developed into a battle between Dizzy Dean and Cincinnati's Tony Freitas, each of whom pitched 17 innings. Pitch counts weren't kept, but Dean faced an incredible 75 batters. The score was 5-5 after nine innings, and the tie wasn't broken until the 17th when Joe Medwick broke an 0-for-19 slump with a solo home run that struck the top of the left field wall and bounced onto the roof of a laundry building across the street. The Reds tied it again 6-6 in the bottom of the inning. In the 18th, the Cards scored twice off Paul Derringer to take an 8-6 lead on RBI singles by Jack Rothrock and Frankie Frisch, but the Reds rallied in their half off Jim Lindsey, who relieved Dean. Medwick ended the game with a leaping one-handed catch in front of the scoreboard off Jim Bottomley's drive. If Medwick had missed the ball, all three runs would have scored. The second game resulted in a 2-2 tie, called after five innings by darkness.

Cardinals

02
July

On this date in 1951, Bill Veeck assumed control of the St. Louis Browns from Bill and Charles DeWitt. Veeck was highly successful as owner of the Cleveland Indians from 1946 through 1949. The club won its first pennant in 28 years in 1948 and drew 2.6 million fans, a major league attendance record that stood until 1962. Veeck hoped to breathe life into a floundering, comatose Browns franchise by employing the same crowd-pleasing gimmicks he had used in Cleveland (see August 19). The Browns drew only 247,131 fans in 1950 amid rumors that the club was moving to Baltimore, Milwaukee, Houston or Los Angeles. There were 18 minor league clubs that had higher attendance than the Browns that season. Upon buying the club, Veeck told reporters he had no plans to pull the Browns out of St. Louis. Veeck's intention was to promote the Browns and run the Cardinals out of town, leaving St. Louis all to himself. Of course, he was unsuccessful in achieving that goal.

Cardinals

03
July

On this date in 1995, Mike Morgan pitched 8⅓ innings of no-hit baseball against the Expos at Busch Stadium. In the final frame, he induced Curtis Pride to fly out, and fans began to believe they were about to witness an historic feat. Morgan then walked Tony Tarasco. With one out and one on base, he faced Will Cordero, who nubbed a grounder to Scott Cooper, who rushed in and grabbed the ball but threw it past first base. Cordero sped to second base, and the play was ruled a hit and an error. Morgan was pulled from the game, as Jeff Parrett closed it out. Losing the no-hitter on such an excuse-me hit must have been tough for Morgan, but he certainly must have been used to bad luck. During his 22-year career, Morgan compiled a respectable 4.23 ERA—not great but good enough to keep him in the majors for a long career. But that ERA earned him a rather bleak lifetime won-loss record of 141-186—45 games under .500! It also earned him quite a few changes of uniform. He was the quintessential journeyman, setting a major league record by playing for 12 teams during his MLB career.

Cardinals

04
July

On this date in 1906, the Cardinals spilt a raucous doubleheader with the Reds in St. Louis. The Cards lost the first game 12-0 and won the second 2-1 in ten innings. Fans shot toy pistols into the air during the games and threw firecrackers at Cincinnati left fielder Joe Kelley, who at times was obscured by a cloud of smoke. During the late 19th and early 20th centuries, it wasn't unusual for fans to attend July 4 doubleheaders with toy pistols, firecrackers and fireworks to celebrate the occasion. In 1903, the American Medical Association began tracking deaths and injuries on July 4 and was appalled by the findings. From 1903 through 1909, 1,360 Americans died on the holiday from accidents, an average of 170 a year, mostly from fireworks and firearms, with a peak of 213 in 1909. Beginning in 1911, government agencies and newspapers campaigned to urge Americans to practice a "safe and sane" holiday. Toy pistols, fireworks and cannons were outlawed in many cities and towns. The crusade spread rapidly, and the deaths dropped to 41 in 1912.

Cardinals

05
July

On this date in 1955, Cardinals manager Harry Walker and Reds manager Birdie Tebbetts fought each other at home plate during a 5-4 Cardinals loss in Cincinnati. Tebbetts complained to umpire Jocko Conlan about the Cardinals' stalling tactics with the score tied 4-4 in the bottom of the ninth. When Walker joined in the discussion, Tebbetts stepped around Conlan and swung at the St. Louis skipper. The two managers wrestled each other to the ground, while both benches emptied and fights erupted all over the field. After the field was cleared of combatants, Johnny Temple drove in the winning run with a single. Tebbetts and Walker were ejected and fined $100 by the league office.

Cardinals

06
July

After losing the first game of a doubleheader 6-0 against the Cubs in Chicago on this date in 1913, the Cardinals won the second contest by forfeit. By prior agreement, the second game was to end at 5:00 p.m. to allow both teams to catch a train. After the Cardinals took a 3-0 lead in the third, the club began to make outs deliberately in order to keep the game moving so that five innings could be played before 5:00 p.m. and thereby make the game official. The Cubs, on the other hand, stalled as much as possible. The last straw for umpire Mal Eason was a play in which Cards catcher Ivy Wingo bunted to Cubs pitcher Ed Reulbach, who threw the ball wildly to first base. Second baseman Johnny Evers, who was also the Cubs manager, retrieved it and made no attempt to retire Wingo, who slowly trotted around the bases. Eason declared the contest a forfeit. Outraged, Evers punched Eason but somehow escaped suspension from the league office.

Cardinals

07
July

After being released by the Cubs, Dizzy Dean signed with St. Louis radio station KWK as a broadcaster of Cardinals and Browns games on this date in 1941. He did the color with Johnny O'Hara on the play-by-play. When the Cardinals and Browns broadcasts were split in 1947 and each team had its own set of announcers, Dean did the Browns games exclusively. Dean's broadcasting career included the infancy of television and lasted into the 1960s. With his use of malapropisms, humorous stories and fracturing of the English language, Dean was enormously popular behind the mic and announced the National Game of the Week on CBS television during the 1950s. Though he was, without question, a national celebrity during his playing days, he enjoyed even greater fame throughout the country during his time as an announcer.

Cardinals

08
July

On this date in 1901, an eighth-inning decision by umpire Hank O'Day infuriated the crowd in St. Louis. When the contest resulted in a 7-6 Dodgers win over the Cardinals, hundreds of fans rushed at O'Day, who suffered a split lip before police, with revolvers drawn, could rescue him. The crowd milled around after the contest for an hour, and O'Day needed police protection to move from his dressing room to a waiting police carriage. While the carriage was stalled in traffic on the way to O'Day's hotel, the umpire was recognized and pelted with stones. Once again, police drew their revolvers to quell the disturbance. O'Day couldn't make it to the ballpark for the remaining two games of the series because of the injuries he suffered. One player from each team served as a substitute umpire during the two contests.

Cardinals

09
July

Today's trivia: Who held the Cardinals record for most home runs in a season before the arrival of Mark McGwire?

When Mark McGwire belted 70 home runs for the Cardinals in 1998, the previous team record was 43 by Johnny Mize in 1940. No Cardinal batter hit 40 homers or more in a season from 1941 through 1997. Of the 16 franchises in existence during each of those 57 seasons, the Cardinals are the only one without a player hitting at least 40 homers. Each of the other 15 teams had at least three instances of a player clobbering 40 or more. Through 2009, there have been 11 occasions in which a St. Louis hitter belted 40 or more homers in a season. Albert Pujols accomplished the feat five times in 2003, 2004, 2005, 2006 and 2009. The others are by McGwire (1997 and 1998), Jim Edmonds (2000 and 2004), Mize (1940) and Rogers Hornsby (1922). Hornsby was the first player other than Babe Ruth to hit at least 40 homers in a season. Ruth set the season record with 29 as a member of the Red Sox in 1919, shattering that mark with 54 as a Yankee in 1920, then struck 59 more in 1921.

Cardinals

10
July

Enforcing a law barring business on Sundays, St. Louis police stopped the game against Baltimore at Sportsman's Park on this date in 1887. The law was enacted in 1839 by the Missouri legislature to prevent business or "labor" from being conducted on Sundays but exempted places of amusement. The Cardinals had played on Sundays since 1882 as a "place of amusement," but many in the community disagreed, claiming baseball was a "business," and they organized efforts to stop it. Police had warned club owner Chris Von der Ahe of arrests if the July 10 game was played, but he announced the contest would start as scheduled. Some 12,000 were present, and at the opening of the second inning, a police sergeant stepped forward and informed Von Der Ahe that he was under arrest for violating the Sunday law. The crowd booed and many broke onto the field, but umpire Bob Ferguson kept the game going for several minutes before he was threatened with arrest. At this point, Ferguson called off the game. The fans were given "rain checks" to use for another contest later in the season. On July 15, a judge ruled that the Cardinals could continue playing on Sundays in the future without interference from law enforcement officials.

Cardinals

11
July

On this date in 1911, the Cardinals survived a deadly train wreck at 3:35 a.m. on the New York, New Haven & Hartford Railroad. Running from Washington to Boston, the train crashed into a viaduct and plunged down an 18-foot embankment 1½ miles west of Bridgeport, Connecticut, killing 14 people and injuring 47 others. The cause of the accident was attributed to the engineer, who tried to negotiate a switch at a high speed. After realizing that none of their teammates was injured, the Cardinals players labored in the midst of the wreckage until the last body was pulled out 15 hours later. Ironically, the Pullman sleeping car of the St. Louis team was repositioned from near the front of the train to a spot near the rear shortly before the wreck because manager Roger Bresnahan complained that his players couldn't sleep due to engine noise after the club boarded the train in Philadelphia. The day coach, which took the place of the Pullman car in which the Cardinals were riding, was so badly crushed and splintered that it was unrecognizable. Most of those who died in the accident were riding in the day coach. The railroad paid the players $25 apiece for their efforts and their lost possessions.

Cardinals

12
July

During a doubleheader on this date in 1931, the Cardinals and Cubs combined for a record 32 doubles, 23 of them in the second game. The twin bill attracted a record crowd of 45,715 at the St. Louis ballpark, about 13,000 more than the stands could accommodate. The remainder encircled the outfield. The Cubs couldn't take infield practice because the mob stole the balls. The start of the first game was delayed as fans wandered around the field overwhelming the ushers and law enforcement officials. When police were successful in pushing the crowd back in one area, it would surge forward in another. The game started with spectators in fair territory only 70 feet behind first base, about 100 feet behind third and not more than 150 feet behind second. Balls hit into the overflow during the two games were ground rule doubles, which contributed mightily to the record number of two-baggers, many of which were pop flies. The throng turned the game into a farce. Outfielders practically played on the heels of the infielders. The Cubs won the first game 8-5 with nine doubles in the contest, five of them by Chicago batters.

Cardinals

13
July

The question of the day: What happened in the second game of the July 12, 1931, doubleheader between the Cardinals and the Cubs in St. Louis?

Between the two games, the crowd occupied the entire field, and it had to be cleared again. This time the fans edged a few feet closer to the infield, further squeezing the playing area. The Cardinals bounced back in the second contest, winning 17-13. St. Louis scored seven runs in the second inning to take a 10-6 lead, and after the Cubs tied it 10-10 with four runs in the fifth, the Cards broke the deadlock with three in their half. There were 23 doubles, the most ever by two teams in a single game. The 13 doubles by the Cards is the most by a club in a single game since 1900. The Cards also set an all-time major league record for most doubles in a doubleheader with 17. The 17 doubles were by Ripper Collins (four), Gus Mancuso (three), Chick Hafey (two), Frankie Frisch (two), Ernie Orsatti (two), George Watkins (two), Andy High (one) and Jake Flowers (one).

Cardinals

14
July

The new Busch Stadium hosted the All-Star Game on this date in 2009. The American League won 4-3. Excluding the 2002 tie, it was the 12th win in a row for the AL. It was the first All-Star Game in St. Louis since 1966 and the fifth overall. The others were in 1940, 1948 and 1957. With the help of an error by Albert Pujols, the AL scored two runs in the first inning. The NL answered with three tallies in the second. The AL scored in the fifth and the eighth for the win. The go-ahead run crossed the plate on a triple by Curtis Granderson and a sacrifice fly from Adam Jones. Carl Crawford robbed Brad Hawpe of a home run in the seventh inning and was the game's MVP. Barack Obama threw out the ceremonial first pitch and joined Joe Buck and Tim McCarver in the broadcast booth in the second inning. Obama was the first sitting president to attend an All-Star Game since Gerald Ford in Philadelphia in 1976. Obama was the third sitting president to attend a game in St. Louis. The first was William Howard Taft in 1910 and 1911 at Sportsman's Park. The second was George W. Bush on April 5, 2004, at the second Busch Stadium. Bush watched the first five innings from a private box. The Cards lost 8-6 to the Brewers.

Cardinals

15
July

On this date in 1905, Cardinals pitcher Wish Egan gave up back-to-back homers in Boston that traveled several miles, but the Cardinals defeated the Braves 11-8. Just beyond the short left field wall at South End Grounds in Boston, and only about 300 feet from home plate, ran the tracks of the New York, New Haven and Hartford Railroad. Jim Delahanty of the Braves smacked a ball that bounced high and plopped into the gondola car of a moving freight train heading south. Someone finally retrieved the ball when the train reached the end of the line in Willamantic, Connecticut, 75 miles away. Harry Wolverton was the next batter and, incredibly, hit a home run into a northbound passenger train, which traveled another six miles to City Point in South Boston. Egan was later a scout for the Tigers from 1910 through 1951. Among his discoveries were future Hall of Famers Hal Newhouser, George Kell and Jim Bunning. Egan is also credited with selecting the Tigers spring training site of Lakeland, Florida, in 1933. The relationship between the Tigers and Lakeland is the longest in baseball history between a club and its spring training home. His nickname "Wish" was short for his given name of Aloysius.

Cardinals

16
July

Today's trivia: Who did the Cardinals trade to acquire Willie McGee?

The Cardinals traded pitcher Bob Sykes to the Yankees for Willie McGee on October 21, 1981. It is among the most one-sided trades in club history. McGee was an obscure 23-year-old outfielder when the Cardinals acquired him, and he had yet to play above the Class AA level. The quiet, unassuming McGee started the 1982 season in the minors but was called up during the second week of May after an injury to David Green. McGee made his presence felt by batting .296 in 123 games as a rookie and fit right in with the need for speed and line drive hitting at Busch Stadium. In 12 seasons with the club from 1982 through 1990 and again from 1996 through 1999, he played in 1,549 games. McGee was the MVP in 1985 when he led the NL in batting average (.353), triples (18) and hits (216). He also led the NL in batting average in 1990 with a mark of .335. Oddly, McGee was traded to the A's on August 29 of that year, but accumulated enough plate appearances before leaving St. Louis to qualify for the batting title. After being traded by the Cardinals, Bob Sykes never appeared in another major league game.

Cardinals

17
July

On this date in 1961, Bill White collected eight hits in ten at-bats during a doubleheader sweep of the Cubs at Busch Stadium. In the opener, White had four singles in five at-bats. Down 6-0, the Cards scored four runs in the seventh inning and six in the eighth for a 10-6 win. In the nightcap, White was four-for-five again with a double and three singles. The Redbirds won 8-5. White continued his torrid hitting the next day with six hits in eight at-bats during 8-3 and 7-5 triumphs over the Cubs in another double-header in St. Louis. White was three-for-four in each game. He had a homer and two singles in the first contest and two triples and a single in the second skirmish. With 14 hits in 18 at-bats on July 17 and 18, White tied a major league record set by Ty Cobb for most hits in consecutive doubleheaders. Cobb's feat came on July 17 and 19, 1912, almost 49 years to the day before White's. White started the streak on the day that Cobb died at the age of 74 in Atlanta. There was a moment of silence prior to the July 18 twin bill in Cobb's honor. On July 19, White was the hero again with a walk-off single in the tenth inning that defeated the Giants 3-2 at Busch Stadium.

Cardinals

18
July

On this date in 1994, the Cardinals blew an 11-run lead and lost 15-12 to the Astros at the Astrodome. St. Louis took an 11-0 lead with three runs in the first inning, four in the second, and four in the third. Houston rallied, however, by scoring two runs in the fourth, two in the fifth and 11 in the sixth before the Cards scored a meaningless run in the ninth. The Astros orchestrated their comeback against pitchers Allen Watson, Frank Cimorelli, Brian Eversgerd and Steve Dixon. The 11-run comeback tied a National League record for the largest deficit overcome to win a game. The Cardinals came from 11 back to beat the Giants 14-12 in New York on June 15, 1952, and the Phillies trailed 12-1 before beating the Cubs 18-16 in ten innings on April 17, 1976, in Chicago. Dixon pitched only six major league games over two seasons. In five innings, he walked 13 batters and allowed 16 runs for an ERA of 28.80. Cimorelli's career lasted only 11 games and he never pitched another big league game after July 18, 1994.

Cardinals

19
July

Today's trivia: When was the only All-Star Game played at the second Busch Stadium?

The second Busch Stadium hosted its only All-Star Game two months after it opened on July 12, 1966, before a crowd of 49,936, and the National League won 2-1 in ten innings on a day in which the official high temperature in St. Louis hit 105 degrees. Hundreds of fans in the field level boxes left their seats, at least temporarily, because of the broiling sun. The heat resulted in more than 130 people requiring first aid care at the stadium. Asked to comment about the new stadium, which opened two months earlier on May 12, Casey Stengel said that it "certainly holds the heat well." The winning run in the tenth inning scored when Tim McCarver singled, moved to second on a sacrifice from Ron Hunt, and crossed the plate on a single by Maury Wills. Denny McLain was the AL starting pitcher and retired all nine batters he faced over three innings. The NL pitchers were Sandy Koufax (three innings), Jim Bunning (two innings), Juan Marichal (three innings) and Gaylord Perry (two innings).

Cardinals

20
July

On this date in 1947, the Dodgers scored three runs in the ninth inning to defeat the Cardinals 3-2 at Ebbets Field. The game was later wiped off the books because of the Cardinals' protest. In the ninth inning with two outs and two Cardinals on base, umpire Beans Reardon signaled that the drive of St. Louis outfielder Ron Northey had gone into the stands for a home run. Northey slowed down to a jog on his trip around the bases. Northey arrived at the plate to find catcher Bruce Edwards waiting for him with ball in hand. The umpires conferred and ruled that the ball struck the top of the wall and that Northey was out. After the game was over, the Cardinals filed a protest with NL president Ford Frick. After deliberation, Frick ruled that the game should go into the books as a 3-3 tie and that Northey should be credited with a homer. The contest was replayed on August 18, with the Dodgers winning 12-3. The proceeds of the replayed game totaled $46,000 and went toward the erection of the memorial to World War II veterans in Brooklyn. The memorial was dedicated in 1951 in Brooklyn's Cadman Plaza.

21
July

On this date in 1977, August Busch lifted the ban on facial hair for the rest of the season while extending manager Vern Rapp's contract one more year through the end of 1978. Rapp and his players had been in almost constant disagreement over the manager's grooming edicts since the first day of spring training. Al Hrabosky was at the forefront of the controversy because he believed that his Fu Manchu mustache intimidated hitters and was necessary for him to pitch well. At the time Busch allowed him to grow the mustache again, Hrabosky had been cuffed around by National League hitters all season. Busch read a long statement to the press, and indirectly at Hrabosky, at the time of the announcement: "You said in the newspaper that you can only get batters out by being psyched up with your mustache and beard. Then go ahead and grow it. But, boy are you going to look like a fool if you don't get batters out.... You painted me into a corner and no one does that to me." The *St. Louis Post-Dispatch* ran a daily "Hair Meter" for weeks afterward showing Al's stats after he grew back his beard. For the record, there was little noticeable difference in Hrabosky's pitching record with or without the beard during the 1977 season. At the end of the season, he was traded to the Kansas City Royals.

22
July

On this date in 1903, Cardinals outfielder Homer Smoot beat the Reds 8-7 in St. Louis with a three-run, inside-the-park homer in the ninth inning. With two out and two strikes, Smoot hit a drive to right field. With the sun setting, Cincinnati outfielder Cozy Dolan didn't see the ball in the darkness and stood still as a statue while the ball sailed past him. First baseman Jake Beckley had to retrieve the ball, but by the time he tracked it down, Smoot had scored. Reds pitcher Jack Harper angrily picked up the ball and heaved it into the stands as fans poured onto the field and carried Smoot around the diamond on their shoulders.

23
July

The question of the day: What happened during the 1885 World Series?

From 1884 through 1890, the American Association champion played the National League champion in a World Series to determine the world champion. The Cardinals won the AA pennant each year from 1885 through 1888, and thus played in four consecutive World Series. In 1885, the Cardinals met the Chicago White Stockings, a franchise known today as the Cubs. (The Cubs nickname was attached to the team for the first time in 1902.) The series was scheduled for seven games, with two in Chicago, three in St. Louis, one in Pittsburgh and one in Cincinnati. The Cards won game seven 13-4 in Cincinnati to claim the title. But game two remained in dispute. Chicago manager Cap Anson pulled his team off the field objecting to the calls of umpire David Sullivan, who forfeited the game to the Cardinals. After the series ended, Anson decided the forfeit should be thrown out, and a select committee agreed, leaving the series in a draw with each team winning three games. The Cardinals and White Stockings split the prize money of $1,000.

Cardinals

24
July

The question of the day: What happened during the 1886 World Series?

The Cardinals and White Stockings met again in the 1886 World Series, which was set again as a best-of-seven affair, with the winner taking all of the prize money. The Cards won four games to two with game six resulting in a ten-inning, 4-3 victory in St. Louis. The winning run scored when Chicago pitcher John Clarkson threw the ball past catcher King Kelly and Curt Welch raced in from third base. Contemporary newspapers differ on exactly what took place when Welch scored the winning run. Some called it a passed ball, others a wild pitch. There is also a dispute over when Welch broke for the plate. Did he move forward after the ball sailed past the catcher, or did he break with the pitch in attempt to steal? There is also disagreement over whether Welch slid across the plate or went in standing. Regardless, the play has gone into history as the "$15,000 slide," an amount slightly above the $13,920.10 in prize claimed by the Cardinals.

25
July

The question of the day: What happened in the 1887 World Series.

The Cardinals played the National League champion Detroit Wolverines in the 1887 World Series. The owners of the two clubs agreed to a 15-games series played in ten different cities over 17 days. All 15 games were to be played regardless of the outcome. The ten cities were St. Louis, Detroit, Pittsburgh, Brooklyn, New York, Boston, Philadelphia, Washington, Baltimore and Chicago. In game 11 at the Swampdoodle Grounds in Washington, Detroit won 13-2 for their eighth victory, sealing the championship. The final four games went off as scheduled, and each club won two. Game 15 drew only 859 fans in St. Louis. Expressing his displeasure with losing, owner Chris Von der Ahe refused to pay his players for the postseason. On October 30, the Cardinals embarked on a long barnstorming tour that lasted until February. The club played the Chicago White Stockings in Charleston, Atlanta, Memphis, Nashville, New Orleans, and several Texas, New Mexico and Arizona towns before reaching San Francisco for a series of contests.

Cardinals

26
July

The question of the day: What happened during the 1888 World Series?

The Cardinals played the New York Giants in the 1888 World Series. The clubs agreed to an 11-games series. Two contests were scheduled for Brooklyn and Philadelphia. The Giants won five of the first six games. On the travel day between games six and seven, charges that umpires John Kelly and John Gaffney had wagered on the Giants were attributed to Chris Von der Ahe and were reported by the Associated Press. Both umpires threatened to sit out the rest of the series. Von der Ahe claimed he was misquoted and affirmed the honesty of the umpires. The Giants wrapped up the series with their six victory in game eight, and the final three games were played as scheduled, including two in St. Louis which drew "crowds" of 711 and 412. The Cards won each of the final three contests. After losing the series, Von der Ahe called his team "chumps," and for the second straight year refused to pay his players for participating in the World Series.

Cardinals

27
July

On this date in 1927, pitcher Flint Rhem left the club after being fined $2,500 during a road trip. Rhem had a 20-7 record in 1926, but was constantly in trouble with club management for his drunken behavior. His contract in 1927 called for a bonus of $2,500 if he didn't take a drink during the season. Rhem forfeited the bonus when he got drunk at the Elk's Club in Boston, which recently had been converted into a hotel. Despite the laws of prohibition, a nightclub had been set up on the third floor, and in violation of club rules, Rhem, Grover Alexander and others partied late into the night and by morning were in a drunken stupor. Citing that others were involved in the indiscretion, Rhem asked: "Why should I be penalized for enjoying myself on a trip?" He also came up with the lame excuse that he drank the booze to keep it away from Alexander, who was a noted alcoholic. "They were passing drinks to Alex so fast, I had to drink 'em up," said Rhem. "I wanted to keep him sober. He's more important to the club than I am." Rhem returned to the club four days later when owner Sam Breadon gave him $500 of his $2,500 abstinence bonus because he made it to July without taking a drink. Rhem was 105-97 during a 12-year career, ten of them with the Cardinals. He continued to struggle with alcoholism until his career ended in 1936.

Cardinals

28
July

The question of the day: When was Flint Rhem "kidnapped?"

During a heated pennant race, Flint Rhem was scheduled to start against the Dodgers in Brooklyn on September 17, 1930, but he had disappeared for 48 hours before showing up at the ballpark bleary-eyed, hung over, and in no condition to pitch. He covered his tracks with an outlandish tale. Rhem claimed he had been standing in front of the Cardinals' hotel in Manhattan when two men called him over to a limousine. Flint said he walked over, and the pair pushed him into the vehicle and pointed a gun. The men drove him to New Jersey, and forced him to drink raw whiskey. According to Rhem, the kidnappers were gamblers and threatened him with bodily harm if he pitched and won his start against the Dodgers. Cardinal management was skeptical, but called police. Rhem couldn't find the place in New Jersey where he was taken, however, and law enforcement officials dropped the pursuit of the "abductors."

Cardinals

29
July

On this date in 1884, Cardinals pitcher Dave Foutz made his major league debut and struck out 13 batters in a 13-inning, 6-5 win over the Reds in Cincinnati. Foutz left his native Maryland in the late 1870s to seek a fortune as a gold miner in Leadville, Colorado. Pitching for the Leadville nine, he posted a 40-1 record and caught the attention of major league scouts. Standing six-foot-two and weighing 165 pounds, Foutz was nick-named "Scissors" and "His Needles." In his first 20 days in St. Louis, he pitched in ten games and won eight of them before being put out of action for three weeks in late August and early September with malarial fever. Foutz recovered from the ailment to forge an excellent career. In four seasons in St. Louis, he had a record of 114-48. Among Cardinals pitchers with at least 100 decisions and 1,000 innings, Foutz ranks first in winning percentage (.704) and second in ERA (2.67). He also rates fourth in complete games (156 in 166 starts). A broken thumb suffered in August 1887 curtailed his pitching effectiveness, and at the end of the season, Foutz was dealt to the Brooklyn Dodgers, where he played nine seasons as a hard-hitting first baseman and outfielder. He was only 40 when he died of asthma in 1897.

Cardinals

30
July

The question of the day: Along with Dave Foutz (see yesterday's entry) what other St. Louis pitcher-out-fielder made his debut in 1884?

Six weeks after Foutz made his major league debut, the Cardinals unveiled 20-year-old pitcher Bob Caruthers. Foutz and Caruthers were a potent 1-2 punch at the top of the rotation for the Cardinals' 1885, 1886 and 1887 pennant-winning teams. The son of a wealthy Memphis doctor, Caruthers stood only five-foot-seven and weighed just 138 pounds. Despite his small stature, he had a 108-48 record with the Cardinals and ranks third in club history in winning percentage. Caruthers was an excellent hitter and often played the outfield between starts. He had a career batting average of .282. On March 13, 1886, Caruthers agreed to a salary of $3,200 for the upcoming season, conducting negotiations with owner Chris Von Der Ahe via transatlantic telegraph. Caruthers was on a trip to Paris with teammate Doc Bushong. Von Der Ahe blamed Caruthers and his love of the nightlife for the loss to the Detroit Wolverines in the 1887 World Series, and sold Caruthers to the Dodgers in November. He continued his fine pitching, and finished his career with a record of 218-99.

Cardinals

31
July

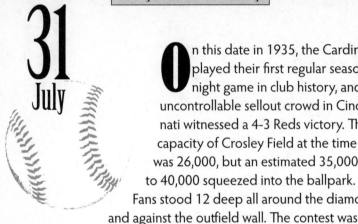

On this date in 1935, the Cardinals played their first regular season night game in club history, and an uncontrollable sellout crowd in Cincinnati witnessed a 4-3 Reds victory. The capacity of Crosley Field at the time was 26,000, but an estimated 35,000 to 40,000 squeezed into the ballpark. Fans stood 12 deep all around the diamond and against the outfield wall. The contest was delayed for 25 minutes in the third inning when many of the unruly fans scampered across the outfield. Order was restored by the riot squad of the Cincinnati police and the threat of a forfeit to the Cardinals. Players couldn't see the action from the dugout and had difficulty making their way to the playing field through the crush of fans. The managers had to call out to fans to find out what was happening on the field. In the eighth, when play was stopped to tend to an injured player, Kitty Burke, a young woman in the crowd near home plate, grabbed the bat from the hands of Reds outfielder Babe Herman and pranced to the batter's box. Cards pitcher Paul Dean tossed an underhand pitch to Miss Burke, who grounded to first base. She later toured the burlesque circuit as the only woman to "bat" in the major leagues. Somehow in the midst of the pandemonium a baseball game was played. The Reds won it on a walk-off single by Billy Sullivan.

Cardinals

August

Cardinals

01
August

On this date in 1971, the Cardinals scored three runs in the 12th inning to take a 6-3 lead over the Phillies before rain halted play in a bizarre game in Philadelphia. Rain suspended play for an hour and 48 minutes in the top of the 12th with the score 3-3 and two Cards on base. Play resumed and the Cardinals scored three times. Rain then stopped play for 31 minutes, and the umpires finally called off the game. According to league rules then in force, the score reverted back to the last full inning played, which meant the contest went into the books as an 11-inning, 3-3 tie. The Cardinals filed a protest and claimed the Phillies failed to put the playing field back into condition after the rain stopped. NL president Chub Feeney upheld the protest because of mechanical failure of the Zamboni that removed water from the artificial surface at Veterans Stadium. Debris blown onto the field during the storm clogged the machine. Feeney ruled the game suspended with the Cardinals leading 6-3. It was completed on September 7. The Phillies rallied for three runs in the bottom of the 12th to tie the score 6-6 before the Cardinals scored three in the 13th to win 9-6.

Cardinals

02 August

On this date in 1938, the Cardinals and Dodgers experimented with dandelion yellow baseballs during a 6-2 Brooklyn win in the first game of a doubleheader at Ebbets Field. The switch to a conventional white ball in the second tilt failed to aid the Cards as the Dodgers won again, 9-3. The motivating force behind the yellow ball was scientist Frederick Rahr, who made an agreement with the Spalding Baseball Company to manufacture the balls. Rahr believed that its high visibility would lessen the danger of batters being hit by pitched balls. Larry MacPhail, Brooklyn's general manager, took it from there and persuaded NL president Ford Frick and the Cardinal management team of Sam Breadon and Branch Rickey to sanction the test. Player reaction was mixed, but most agreed that the ball was easier to follow. One drawback surfaced when the yellow dye came off on the hands of the pitchers. The entire side of the uniform of Dodgers hurler Fred Fitzsimmons was stained where he wiped off the dye. Yellow balls were used again for two Cardinals-Dodgers games in 1939 and another between the Dodgers and Cubs, but the experiment was never tried again. In 1970, Oakland A's owner Charlie Finley advocated the use of orange baseballs, and tried it out in an exhibition game, but he failed to gain the interest of his fellow owners.

Cardinals

03
August

The question of the day: Why did singer Jose Feliciano create controversy during the 1968 World Series between the Cardinals and the Tigers?

Jose Feliciano, a blind 23-year-old Puerto Rican folk singer, created a firestorm when he sang the National Anthem on national television at Tigers Stadium before game five. Feliciano's interpretation was done to a slower beat in a blend of soul and folk styles with an acoustic guitar, and it differed greatly from the normal rendition. At a time when the country was bitterly divided over the Vietnam War, newspapers and radio and television stations were flooded with protests by irate viewers, many of whom considered the performance to be unpatriotic. Today, Feliciano's rendition would barely raise an eyebrow, as individual expressions of "The Star-Spangled Banner" have become commonplace and the lyrics have been sung in a wide variety of musical styles since his groundbreaking performance.

Cardinals

04
August

Rookie Bill Pertica pitched the Cardinals to a raucous 1-0 win over the Giants at Sportsman's Park on this date in 1921. In the eighth inning, New York hurler Art Nehf hit Joe Schultz in the head with a pitch. While Schultz was being revived, a remark by Cardinals catcher Pickles Dillhoefer angered Giants receiver Frank Snyder, and several blows were exchanged before the umpires separated them. Both were ejected. When Snyder left the New York bench shortly afterward, fans showered the field with bottles from the stands, and police were called upon to restore order and see the opposing players off the field safely. Dillhoefer died of typhoid-pneumonia on February 23, 1922, in St. Louis at the age of 27. He was taken ill on January 19, only five days after marrying Massie Slocum, a schoolteacher from Mobile, Alabama. His funeral was held in the same Mobile church where he was married six weeks earlier.

05
August

Jesse Haines died on this date in 1978. He pitched for the Cardinals from 1920 through 1937 and pitched his last game at the age of 44. Haines ranks second among Cardinals pitchers in career wins (210), first in games (554), third in games started (388), second in complete games (209), fifth in shutouts (24), second in innings pitched (3,203⅔) and fifth in strikeouts (979). Haines was elected to the Hall of Fame in 1970. He also pitched a no-hitter to defeat the Boston Braves 5-0 at Sportsman's Park on July 17, 1924. It was the first no-hitter by a Cardinal pitcher since 1891 and the first since the club joined the National League a year later. Haines walked three and fanned five. In the ninth inning, he retired Gus Felix on a fly ball to Jack Smith in right field, a pop-up by Bill Cunningham to Jimmy Cooney at shortstop, and Casey Stengel on a grounder to Rogers Hornsby at second. The no-hitter was pitched on Tuberculosis Day, an annual event at Sportsman's Park that was staged to benefit the efforts of the St. Louis Tuberculosis Society to eradicate the disease. The benefit took place each year from 1915 through 1942.

06
August

The question of the day: How did Chris Von der Ahe attempt to make additional money by renting out his ballpark in 1893?

Von der Ahe believed he could make money by scheduling other events while the Cardinals were on the road during the 1893 season. A bicycle race was staged in July, churning up cinder and dust from the track surrounding the field. Players complained about the conditions, and Von der Ahe promised his men a share of the gate receipts from an upcoming Civil War re-enactment called "The Bombardment of Fort Sumter" held during a long road trip in August. Von der Ahe said the amount would reach $2,500. To collect, Cardinal players had to win 20 of their next 40 games. Instead, the club embarked on a long losing streak. The re-enactment was a financial flop. All it accomplished was further destruction of the grounds. Numerous animals traipsed around the field, leaving deep divots, and spent fireworks casings littered the diamond. In 1894, Von der Ahe staged a Wild West Show at the ballpark. The show featured 40 cowboys and 50 full-blooded Sioux Indians. Cardinals manager Doggie Miller even participated to settle a debt he owed to Von der Ahe. The debt was wiped out when Miller agreed to shoot blanks from a Winchester at stage coach-robbing Sioux.

Cardinals

07
August

The question of the day: When did Chris Von der Ahe open a racetrack at New Sportsman's Park? In yet another money-making scheme, Von der Ahe opened a race track on September 30, 1895. Portions of the left and right field bleachers were altered and the grass sod torn up in a circle around the yard. One straightaway was beyond the outfield and the other behind home plate. The reconfigured grounds contained another bar so that patrons could enjoy an alcoholic beverage while placing a bet. Sportswriters and fellow National League owners were outraged at the combination baseball park and race track but were powerless to stop Von der Ahe from carrying out the plan since the races were held after baseball season was over. The new configuration was filled with festive flags and contained a flower garden and beer pavilion near right field. The grandstands, painted salmon-pink, were lined with geranium beds.

Cardinals

08
August

The question of the day: What did Chris Von der Ahe add to New Sportsman's Park before the start of the 1896 season?

Von der Ahe wasn't finished. Before the 1896 season began he added other amusements and referred to his ballpark at the corner of Vandeveter and Natural Bridge as the "Coney Island of the West." A water-chute ride was built behind the left field wall that patrons in boats could slide down into an artificial lake. A section of the fence was missing, and a batted ball could travel through the opening and roll more than 600 feet into the lake. In the winter, the 750-foot-by-250-foot lake accommodated ice skaters. The ride lasted only two seasons, however. Like most of Von der Ahe's financial ventures during the 1890s, it failed to recoup the cost of construction. The firm that built the contraption sued him for non-payment, and another company that invented the ride took him to court over patent infringement.

Cardinals

09
August

On this date in 2007, former pitcher Rick Ankiel returned to the majors as an outfielder after a three-year absence and hit a three-run homer during a 5-0 win over the Padres at Busch Stadium. Ankiel was 11-7 as a 20-year-old pitcher in 2000, but he developed severe control problems and never returned to form. In 2001, Ankiel walked 25 batters in 24 innings. He spent most of the 2001 through 2004 period in the minors. In the spring of 2005, he announced he was going to make it back to the majors as an outfielder. At Class AAA Memphis in 2007, Ankiel batted .267 with 32 homers and 89 RBIs, earning a recall to the Cards. With his home run on August 9, 2007, he became only the third player in the last 90 years to hit his first major league homers as a pitcher, then hit another as a position player. The other two were Babe Ruth with the Red Sox in 1918 and Clint Hartung of the 1947 Giants. In his first 23 games with the Redbirds in 2007, Ankiel batted .358 with nine homers and 29 RBIs. He played in 120 games for the Cards in 2008 and another 122 in 2009 before going to the Royals as a free agent in 2010. He was traded to the Braves later in the year and became a free agent when the season ended. He then signed on with the Nationals.

Cardinals

10 August

On this date in 2010, the Cardinals got into a melee with the Reds in Cincinnati that was one of the biggest brawls in recent team history. The two teams had been battling throughout the broiling summer months in a very close race for Central Division supremacy, setting up a showdown series in which tensions ran high. The tensions boiled over after Reds shortstop Brandon Phillips made some insulting remarks about the Cardinals that were quoted in a Dayton, Ohio, newspaper and then made national news as the series got underway. When Phillips led off the bottom of the first inning, Cardinals catcher Yadier Molina offered a few words of his own and quickly the pair stood nose to nose. The benches cleared as fights broke out all around home plate. Tempers seemed to calm after a few minutes, but then managers Tony La Russa and Dusty Baker began shouting at each other, and the brouhaha boiled over again. Players pushed into a swarm that roiled all the way to the backstop, where several players were pinned against the net. Reds pitcher Johnny Cueto, who was literally pinned off his feet, kicked wildly to free himself and cracked Cardinals catcher Jason LaRue in the head, causing a concussion. Later that year LaRue retired from baseball. A number of fines and suspensions were handed out and tensions between the clubs continued to simmer for the rest of the season.

Cardinals

11
August

On this date in 1889, the Cardinals took a 2½-game lead over the Dodgers in the American Association pennant race with a 14-4 win before 16,000 at Sportsman's Park. During the 19th century, only one umpire worked at a typical game, but due to the importance of the Cardinals-Dodgers contest, a second umpire was assigned. The overflow from the grandstand ringed the outfield, and a rule was adopted that any ball hit into the crowd was a double. With one out in the seventh inning, St. Louis outfielder Charlie Duffee knocked the ball over the fence for a home run. The hit caused a scrap that lasted for half an hour. The Dodgers claimed the drive should be a double because of the ground rule. The Cardinals asserted it was a home run because it left the park. Even the umpires couldn't agree, with one ruling a double and the other a home run. The Dodgers finally got their way, and Duffee went to second base. Later, Duffee collided with Brooklyn catcher Bob Clark, who claimed he was injured and couldn't continue. At the time, substitutions couldn't be made without the consent of the opposition and the umpires. Cardinals manager Charlie Comiskey refused to allow Clark to leave the game. Four doctors were called to examine Clark, creating another delay of approximately 30 minutes as hundreds of fans stormed the field. Clark was compelled to stay in the game.

Cardinals

12
August

On this date in 1988, Joe Magrane pitched a one-hitter to beat the Cubs 4-0 at Wrigley Field. Magrane won the NL ERA title in 1988 with a figure of 2.18 in 165⅓ innings. Despite the low earned run average, his offensive support was pathetic, and Magrane had a 5-9 won-lost record. Three of his five wins were shutouts. The five wins are the fewest ever for an ERA leader in either league. The son of a professor in cancer research at Morehead State University, Magrane pitched for the Cards from 1987 through 1993 and was a favorite of sportswriters because he was always ready with an intelligent, quick-witted quip to help fill space in the papers. He was 18-9 with a 2.91 ERA in 1989, but arm trouble short-circuited a promising career. Magrane missed the entire 1991 season and most of 1992. He pitched his last game at the age of 31 and finished his career with a 57-67 record. After his playing days ended, Magrane took his oddball sense of humor into the broadcasting booth, working for the Angels, Rays, ESPN and the Major League Baseball Network. He was also the analyst for NBC's baseball coverage during the 2008 Summer Olympics.

Cardinals

13
August

On this date in 1934, Dizzy and Paul Dean left the Cardinals. After the Dean brothers were losing pitchers in both ends of a doubleheader against the Cubs on August 12, they refused to go to Detroit for an exhibition game. Dizzy was fined $100 and Paul $50 by manager Frankie Frisch. When Frisch refused to rescind the fines, Dizzy declared, "Then me and Paul are through with the Cardinals." The Deans refused to take the field for the August 14 game against the Phillies in St. Louis. Frisch asked for their uniforms and Dizzy ripped his to shreds. Then he destroyed another for the benefit of photographers. (The club billed him $36 for the cost of two new uniforms.) Dizzy was suspended for ten days, but Frisch reduced it to seven. Dizzy requested a hearing with Commissioner Kenesaw Landis, held on August 20. Landis upheld the suspension. Paul was suspended for three days and returned to the club on August 17.

Cardinals

14
August

On this date in 1971, Bob Gibson pitched the only no-hitter of his career, defeating the Pirates 11-0 at Three Rivers Stadium. In the ninth inning, Gibson retired Vic Davalillo on a grounder to Dal Maxvill at shortstop, Al Oliver on an easy roller to Ted Kubiak at second, and Willie Stargell on a called third strike. It was the first no-hitter thrown in Pittsburgh since 1907 and was Gibson's 201st career victory. He walked three and struck out ten. Prior to the performance, Gibson had given up on the notion of pitching a no-hitter. "High-ball pitchers don't throw no-hitters," he often said, "and I'm a high-ball pitcher." Indeed, despite 251 career victories and 56 shutouts, Gibson had relatively few low-hit games in his career. He pitched only one one-hitter and seven two-hitters.

Cardinals

15
August

Today's trivia: What pitcher won three games during the 1946 World Series?

Harry Brecheen beat the Red Sox three times in 1946 while leading the Cardinals to the world championship. He started the second game and allowed four hits to defeat the Sox 3-0 in St. Louis. In game six, Brecheen defeated Boston 4-1 to even the series at three wins for each club. He entered the seventh game as a reliever in the eighth inning with the Cardinals leading 3-1, no one out, and runners on second and third. Brecheen retired the first two batters he faced but allowed a two-run double to Dom DiMaggio to tie the score. The Cards took a 4-3 lead into the bottom of the eighth, however, and Brecheen survived a shaky ninth. After he allowed the first two batters to reach base, he retired three in a row to nail down the world title. Brecheen also pitched in the World Series for the Cards in 1943 and 1944. Overall, he was 4-1 with a 0.85 ERA in 32⅔ innings of Series play. Brecheen had a 133-92 regular-season record in 12 seasons with the Cards. He also was the pitching coach for the Orioles in 1966, a staff that allowed only two runs in a four-game sweep of the Dodgers.

Cardinals

16
August

On this date in 1890, the Cardinals fell behind 9-0 in the second inning against the Philadelphia Athletics at Sportsman's Park, then staged an incredible rally to win 12-11. St. Louis took the lead with four runs in the eighth inning. Philadelphia outfielder Curt Welch, an ex-Cardinal serving as the Athletics' captain during the game, caused a brouhaha late in the game. With St. Louis trailing 9-7 in the seventh, Welch tried to replace pitcher Ed Sewell with Sadie McMahon. Umpire Bob Emslie cited a new substitution rule stating that two designated subs had to be listed on the line-up card before the game. McMahon was not one of them. Welch launched into a tirade and Emslie backed down, allowing McMahon in the game. The decision raised the ire of Cardinals manager Count Campau. Still seething as his club continued to blow a huge lead, Welch caused two long delays in both the eighth and ninth by arguing Emslie's calls. Welch was ejected and replaced in center field by Seward, who re-entered the contest in another illegal substitution. The Cardinals were too exhausted to object to Seward's presence, and the tilt was completed without further incident.

Cardinals

17
August

On this date in 1964, club owner August Busch ousted Bing Devine as general manager by demanding his resignation. Dissatisfied with the team's performance, Busch ordered a shake-up of the front office and replaced Devine with Bob Howsam. Busch was disgruntled over many of Devine's trades and believed the farm system had declined. At the time of Devine's dismissal, the Cardinals were in fifth place, nine games behind. He had been an employee of the Cardinals for 25 years and general manager since 1957. Devine was popular with the players, who were angered by his dismissal. Many cited Devine's departure as a catalyst for the incredible comeback that resulted in a world championship in 1964. The Cardinals won largely because of trades by Devine that brought in Lou Brock, Curt Flood, Bill White, Dick Groat, Julian Javier, Curt Simmons and Barney Schultz. Although Busch was upset about what he perceived as a lack of progress in the farm system, the Devine regime signed and developed Steve Carlton, Tim McCarver, Nelson Briles, Ray Sadecki, Mike Shannon, Dal Maxvill and Bobby Tolan. After leaving the Cardinals, Devine worked for the Mets for three years. He returned to the Cardinals as general manager in December 1967 and remained in the post until 1978.

Cardinals

18
August

Cardinal left fielder Cliff Carroll was suspended on this date in 1892 after being involved in a bizarre play during a 13-4 win over Baltimore at Sportsman's Park. Carroll attempted to field a ground ball but misjudged it, and the ball miraculously became lodged in his shirt pocket. Carroll looked around on the ground for the missing ball for a few seconds before locating it. By the time he could extricate the ball, the Oriole runner reached third base. Club owner Chris Von der Ahe was so outraged that he fined Carroll $50 and suspended him without pay for the rest of the season. Carroll appealed the suspension at the end of the season but was denied. The 1892 season was his tenth in the majors. He played one more, with the Boston Braves in 1893.

Cardinals

19
August

In a promotional stunt on this date in 1951, Browns owner Bill Veeck trotted out three-foot-seven-inch, 65-pound Eddie Gaedel to pinch-hit in the first inning of the second game of a doubleheader against the Tigers at Sportsman's Park. Gaedel drew a walk on four pitches. Two days later, American League president Will Harridge barred Gaedel from playing in any future games. In another legendary PR move five days later, the Browns held "Grandstand Manager's Night" at Sportsman's Park. The Browns coaches held up placards for 1,115 fans who voted on options given them, such as setting the line-up, changing pitchers, or positioning the infield by responding with signs that read "yes" or "no." The Browns defeated the Philadelphia Athletics, a rare victory in a season in which the club was 52-102. Cardinals owner Fred Saigh countered Veeck's moves by printing the following line in the club's scorecards: "The Cardinals, a dignified St. Louis institution."

20
August

The question of the day: Who was Frank Lane?

The Cardinals hired 59-year-old Frank Lane as general manger on October 6, 1955. He had worked in the front offices of the Reds and Yankees before becoming general manager of the White Sox at the end of the 1948 season, when the team lost 101 games. With a series of brilliant trades, Lane transformed the Sox from league doormats to pennant contenders. But his volatile personality sparked difficulties with his superiors throughout his career. Lane and White Sox owner Charles Comiskey II bickered constantly, leading to Lane's dismissal in September 1955 even though he had a contract through the 1960 season. Lane went to the Cardinals two weeks after leaving the Sox. With a flurry of deals that included trading fan favorites like Red Schoendienst, Lane helped the Cardinals leap from seventh place in 1955 to second in 1957. He didn't get along any better with August Busch than he had with Charles Comiskey, however, and resigned at the end of the '57 season.

Cardinals

21
August

The question of the day: What incident led to Frank Lane's resignation as general manager of the Cardinals?

August Busch believed that Lane was making too many trades. Lane even tried to deal Stan Musial and Ken Boyer before Busch put a stop to it. Busch and Lane had incompatible visions of the future. Lane believed in the quick fix with rapid-fire trades. Busch wanted a more patient approach by building through the farm system and was upset over Lane's trades that included such young players as Luis Arroyo, Bill Virdon and Jackie Brandt in exchange for veterans past their prime. At a February 1957 dinner of the Knights of the Cauliflower Ear, a St. Louis sportsmen's group, Busch said, "I expect the Cardinals to come close to winning a pennant in 1957, and 1958 is going to have to be a sure thing or Frank Lane will be out on his ass. I mean it." Publicly, Lane dismissed the remark as a joke. Privately, he knew Busch was serious. Lane spent the entire 1957 season looking for another position, and he resigned as general manager of the Cardinals in November to take a similar job with the Indians.

22
August

On this date in 1982, third-string catcher Glenn Brummer pulled off a daring, surprise steal of home in the 12th inning to give the Cardinals a 5-4 win over the Giants at Busch Memorial Stadium. Brummer was in the game only because catcher Gene Tenace had been removed for a pinch-runner and Tenace's substitute, Darrell Porter, had been taken out for a pinch-hitter.

Brummer singled with one out, moved to second on a single by Willie McGee and to third on a two-out infield hit by Ozzie Smith. With David Green batting and Gary Lavelle pitching, Brummer broke for the plate and slid under the tag by Milt May. Brummer ran on his own on a play that clearly violated all the tenets of conventional baseball, but it worked and became one of the catalysts to the Cardinals' drive to the pennant. Brummer stole only four bases in 178 career games. His 1982 teammates gave him a home plate with the autographs of all of the members of the team.

Cardinals

23
August

In his first start with the Cardinals, John Smoltz tied a team record with seven consecutive strikeouts and beat the Padres 5-2 at Petco Park on this date in 2009. It had been 109 years since a Cardinals pitcher accomplished the feat. The only St. Louis pitcher to fan seven in a row was Jack Stivetts on April 27, 1890, when the club was in the American Association and pitchers threw 55 feet from home plate. Smoltz fanned a total of nine in five shutout innings. The strikeout streak started in the first inning when he set down Chase Headley for the third out. In the second, Smoltz struck out Kevin Kouzmanoff, Will Venable and Nick Hundley. In the third, Smoltz fanned Luis Rodriguez, Edward Mujica and Everth Cabrera. Smoltz also had a bunt single and scored the first run of the game. He didn't win another game for the Cards. In seven starts, Smoltz had a 1-3 record and a 4.26 earned run average.

Cardinals

24
August

Today's trivia: What was the St. Louis City Series?

The St. Louis City Series were postseason games between the Cardinals and Browns to determine the "champion" of St. Louis. They were seven-game series played in most seasons from 1903 through 1917. The most famous incident in these series took place during a doubleheader on October 13, 1913.

In the first game, Browns first baseman Del Pratt fielded a ball that took a wicked hop and hit him in the eye. He failed to throw the ball to the pitcher covering first base because he thought the ball was foul. Umpire George Hildebrand called it fair and ruled the runner safe. Pratt rushed toward Hildebrand to argue, igniting jeers from the Cardinals bench. A former football player at the University of Alabama, Pratt sprinted toward the Cardinals dugout and fought with infielder Zinn Beck. After the two were pried apart, Pratt resumed his argument with Hildebrand and was ejected. Meanwhile, the crowd surged onto the field, and the contest was delayed while police cleared the diamond. The remainder of the game went on in peace, with the Cardinals winning 5-2.

Cardinals

25
August

The question of the day: What happened in the second game of the doubleheader against the Browns on October 13, 1913?

The Cardinals victory in the opener evened the series at three wins for each team. The second game would determine the city champion.

After being ejected from the first game, Del Pratt took the field in the second tilt, and the Cardinals objected to his presence in the lineup. Umpires George Hildebrand and Bill Brennan agreed that Pratt was ineligible to play in the second game according to the rules then in force. Browns manager Branch Rickey argued that Pratt should remain, and the umpires walked off the field in disgust. They eventually returned once Rickey agreed to keep Pratt out of the game, but there was only enough time to play five innings before the sun set, and the contest ended with the score 1-1. Due to the ill feeling surrounding the event, the management of both teams agreed to end the series with each team having three victories.

Cardinals

26
August

Whitey Herzog fined shortstop Garry Templeton $5,000 on this date in 1981 for making obscene gestures at fans during a 9-4 win over the Giants at Busch Memorial Stadium. Before the game, Templeton said that he was too tired to play, but Herzog put him in the line-up anyway. Templeton responded with a half-hearted effort. In the first inning, he struck out, but Giants catcher Milt May dropped the ball. Templeton jogged slowly toward first base before veering toward the Cardinal dugout. When the crowd booed, Templeton responded with his middle fingers raised. After two similar gestures later in the game, Templeton was ejected by umpire Bruce Froemming prior to the fourth inning. As Templeton got to the Cardinal dugout, Herzog grabbed him by the shirt and backed him against a wall before players swooped in to break up the scuffle. A day later, Templeton agreed to seek psychiatric help and was hospitalized and treated for what was diagnosed as depression. He returned to the line-up on September 15, but his absence probably cost the Cardinals a berth in the postseason. Mike Ramsey started the 16 games at shortstop that Templeton missed in August and September, and batted only .193 with a slugging percentage of just .211. Templeton hit .288 in 1981 and had a .393 slugging percentage.

Cardinals

27
August

Happy Birthday, Ernie Broglio, who was born on this date in 1935. He had a 21-9 record for the Cardinals in 1960 and was 18-8 in 1963, but he will be remembered largely for being traded by the Cards to the Cubs with Bobby Shantz and Doug Clemens for Lou Brock, Jack Spring and Paul Toth. The Cards came into the 1964 season with high hopes after finishing second in 1963. Those hopes seemed to be dashed early in 1964. Following a June 15 loss to the Astros, the Cards had a 28-31 record and were in eighth place. The offense was anemic with 29 runs in the previous 14 games, 11 of them losses. The corner outfield positions were particularly weak. The Cards had an abundance of pitching, and Broglio was deemed expendable along with Shantz and Clemens to acquire Brock and two marginal pitchers. The trade wasn't well received in St. Louis, however, as most fans believed the Cardinals front office had been bamboozled. Most fans in Chicago were ecstatic, a feeling best summed up by Bob Smith of the *Chicago Daily News* who wrote: "Thank you, thank you, you lovely St. Louis Cardinals," wrote Smith. "Nice doing business with you. Please call again anytime."

Cardinals

28
August

The question of the day: Why did Cardinals fans have an adverse re-action to the trade for Lou Brock?

Ernie Broglio was a proven com-modity. He was 28 years old and had a lifetime record of 70-55. He was 3-5 at the start of the 1964 season but at-tributed his problem to a sore arm and believed the ailment was temporary. Shantz was 38, but he had pitched well for the Cards since being acquired from Houston in 1962. Brock, on the other hand, was viewed as a player who could little but steal a base. He was three days shy of his 25th birthday, had a .257 batting aver-age with just 20 homers in 1,207 at-bats, and was a liability on defense. Within weeks, however, it was apparent to both fans and management alike that the Cardinals had hit a bull's-eye with the trade. Over the remainder of the 1964 season, Brock played in 103 games and batted .348 with 12 homers and 33 stolen bases. He went on to a Hall of Fame career and played in three World Series in St. Louis. In three seasons as a Cub, Broglio had a 7-19 record and a 5.40 ERA.

Cardinals

29

August

On this date in 1977, Lou Brock stole the 892nd and 893rd bases of his career to pass Ty Cobb and break the modern record during a 4-3 loss to the Padres in San Diego. Brock tied the mark with a steal in the first inning. As the first batter of the game, he walked against Dave Freisleben, broke for second on the next pitch, and made it easily as catcher Dave Roberts's throw went into center field. Brock advanced to third where he was mobbed by teammates. The game was halted momentarily while second base was presented to him. He broke the record in the seventh by swiping second with the Cards leading 3-2. Once again, Cardinals surged onto the field to congratulate Brock, who yanked up second base with a big smile and held it aloft. The Padres produced a field mic to allow Brock to address the crowd, which gave him a round of applause. The ceremonies held up the game for five minutes. Brock finished his career in 1979 with 938 steals and held the record until Rickey Henderson passed him in 1991. Henderson ended his career with 1,406 stolen bases. Brock still ranks second.

Cardinals

30
August

On this date in 1955, Stan Musial extended his streak of consecutive games played with a bit of contrivance. It appeared as though his streak would end at 593 games when he was hit on the right hand against the Dodgers the previous day. But in the August 30 game, Musial played only defensively in the bottom of the first inning in a 3-1 loss to the Pirates in Pittsburgh. Listed as sixth in the batting order instead of his usual third slot, Musial was lifted for pinch-hitter Pete Whisenant in the top of the second. On August 31, Musial was in the official starting line-up but never appeared in the game. Whisenant batted for him in the first inning as the Cardinals lost again 4-3 to the Pirates at Forbes Field. Musial's streak ended in 1957 at 895 games.

Cardinals

31
August

On this date in 1988, the Cardinals traded Bob Forsch to the Astros for Denny Walling. Forsch had been a member of the Cardinals since 1974. His greatest day with the club took place on April 16, 1978, when he pitched a no-hitter to beat the Phillies 5-0 at Busch Memorial Stadium with the temperatures hovering in the low 40s. Forsch walked two and struck out three. A controversial scoring decision marred the no-hitter, however. In the eighth inning, a grounder off Garry Maddox's bat slid under third baseman Ken Reitz's glove. It took ten seconds for official scorer Neil Russo of the *St. Louis Post-Dispatch* to rule it an error. The Phillies claimed that Reitz never touched the ball and that it should have been a hit. Reitz said the ball skimmed off his glove and that the play was an error all the way. Bob's brother Ken pitched a no-hitter for the Astros on April 7, 1979. Bob and Ken Forsch are the only pair of brothers in major league history to each record a no-hitter.

Cardinals

September

Cardinals

01
September

Today's trivia: How many law school graduates have managed the Cardinals?

Tony La Russa is the fourth law school graduate to manage the Cardinals. The first three were Miller Huggins (1913–17), Jack Hendricks (1918) and Branch Rickey (1919–25). Huggins graduated from the University of Cincinnati, Hendricks from Northwestern University, Rickey from the University of Michigan and La Russa from Florida State University. There have been only six lawyers to manage in the majors. The other two are Monte Ward (Penn State University) in Providence, New York and Brooklyn during the 1880s and 1890s, and Hughie Jennings (Cornell University) with the Tigers from 1907 through 1920. Of the six lawyers, four are in baseball's Hall of Fame—Huggins, Rickey, Ward and Jennings—and La Russa is a lock to be elected when he becomes eligible. Of the seven lawyers to play in the majors, six were managers. The only non-manager was Muddy Ruel. A native of St. Louis, Ruel attended Soldan High School and Washington University. He played in the big leagues from 1915 through 1934.

Cardinals

02
September

The question of the day: How did Miller Huggins fare as manager of the Cardinals?

Huggins had been a player in the majors since 1904 and a member of the Cardinals since 1910 when named manager on October 22, 1912 at the age of 33. Standing only five-foot-six and weighing 140 pounds, Huggins became a star player with his defense at second base and as a pesky leadoff hitter by drawing walks. He led the NL in walks four times and was in the top five nine seasons from 1904 through 1915. Huggins also ranked among the top five in on-base percentage five times and in runs scored four times. He lasted five seasons as manager of the Cardinals, but had only a 346-415 record with the financially strapped ball club. He tried to buy the Cardinals in 1917 but when the effort failed he resigned as manager. He later managed the Yankees from 1918 until his early death from a skin disease in 1929. Before Huggins arrived, the Yankees had never won an AL pennant. In his 12 seasons at the helm of the club, the Yanks captured six AL pennants and three World Series.

Cardinals

03
September

On this date in 2001, Cardinals rookie Bud Smith pitched a no-hitter to defeat the Padres 4-0 in San Diego. Smith was 21 years old and making his 11th big league start. It was also his first complete game. Smith failed to make it past the seventh inning in his previous starts. He sealed the no-hitter by fielding Phil Nevin's hard comebacker. Smith pumped his fist in the air and ran halfway to first before flipping the ball to Albert Pujols. Smith made 134 pitches, walked four and struck out seven. He finished the 2001 season with a 6-3 record and a 3.63 ERA. He looked to be a star for many years to come but was 1-5 with a 6.94 earned run average in 2002, went to the Phillies in the Scott Rolen trade, and underwent two shoulder surgeries. Ironically, the 134 pitches he threw in the no-hitter might have contributed to the injury problems. Smith's professional career ended in 2007 when he was released by Long Beach, an independent club in the Golden Baseball League. His seven big league victories are tied for the second fewest for a pitcher with a no-hitter. Bobo Holloman, who threw a no-hitter in his first start in the majors for the St. Louis Browns in 1953, had three wins. Like Smith, George Davis of the 1914 Boston Braves had seven career victories.

04
September

On this date in 1887, the Cardinals defeated the New York Metropolitans 18-6 amid chaos in Weehawken, New York. The Metropolitans played a home game in Weehawken because games on Sundays in New York were illegal. The grandstand at Weehawken held only 500 fans, but between 12,000 and 13,000 showed up. The excess ringed the outfield, and there was little police presence to control the crowd. By prior agreement, any ball hit into the crowd was ruled a single. During the first inning, the mob inched forward, making further play impossible. The St. Louis players got in the carriages that had brought them from their hotel in New York and drove around the grounds asking the fans to move back—without success. A horse broke free from one of the carriages and ran through the crowd. After a 30-minute delay, police forced the crowd far enough away from the infield to allow the game to continue, and five more innings were played before darkness ended the contest. The Cardinals brought only nine players from New York to save on transportation expenses. In the fourth inning, Cards outfielder Tip O'Neill let the bat slip out of his hands and it struck teammate Curt Welch in the face. Welch was unable to continue, and the Cardinals finished the game with only eight players.

Cardinals

05
September

Happy Birthday Ernie White, who was born on this date in 1915. In game two of the 1942 World Series against the Yankees, played on October 3 in New York, White pitched a six-hit shutout for a 2-0 win. Spectacular outfield defense helped preserve the victory. With the Cardinals leading 1-0 with one on and two outs in the Yankee half of the sixth, Joe DiMaggio lined a shot into the left-center field gap, but center fielder Terry Moore hauled it in with a diving catch. In the seventh, Joe Gordon drove the ball deep to left, but Stan Musial grabbed it just as it was heading into the seats. Then Charlie Keller blasted the ball to deep right, and Enos Slaughter made a leaping catch at the fence to rob the Yankees of another homer. It was the only postseason game of White's career. He was 17-7 with a 2.40 ERA as a rookie in 1941, but won only 13 games afterward, including a 7-5 mark in 1942. Arm troubles and World War II service shortened his career, which ended with a 30-21 record. No one with fewer career wins has pitched a complete game shutout in the World Series.

Cardinals

06
September

On this date in 1889, the Cardinals lost a controversial 3-2 decision to the Orioles in Baltimore. In the top of the eighth with the Orioles leading 3-2, rain stopped play. After a ten-minute wait, the rain let up, and umpire Fred Goldsmith ordered the teams back on the field. Baltimore manager Billy Barnie protested, preferring to wait until the rain ceased completely. To emphasize the point, Baltimore first baseman Tommy Tucker took the field hoisting an umbrella. Cardinals second baseman Yank Robinson pulled the umbrella down, and Tucker responded by planting his foot in Robinson's posterior. A fight seemed imminent, but Goldsmith and four police officers separated Tucker and Robinson. Before the eighth inning was finished, a downpour ensued and the game was called.

Cardinals

07
September

In the first game of a pennant showdown against the Dodgers in Brooklyn on this date in 1889, the Cardinals lost in a forfeit. The Cardinals led 4-2 in the ninth inning. Player-manager Charlie Comiskey tried to convince umpire Fred Goldsmith that it was too dark to continue, which only aggravated Goldsmith, who had listened to a steady stream of complaints from St. Louis players all day long. Owner Chris Von der Ahe attempted to make his point by buying candles from a nearby grocery store and then lit and arranged them around the St. Louis bench like footlights, which did not improve Goldsmith's mood or that of the Brooklyn fans. Some threw beer steins at the candles. They succeeded in knocking down a number of them, which ignited some stray paper nearby and in turn created a small fire that briefly threatened to set the wooden grandstand ablaze. Fortunately, the flames were extinguished before any real damage was done. Determined to finish the game, Goldsmith ordered the players to begin the ninth. Comiskey refused to play and ordered his team off the field. Goldsmith declared a forfeit in favor of the Dodgers. The crowd of 15,143 cheered the decision. The Cardinals left the field under a barrage of bottles and stones.

Cardinals

08
September

The question of the day: What was the aftermath of the September 7, 1889, forfeit to the Dodgers?

The forfeit dropped the Cardinals 2½ games behind the first-place Dodgers in the American Association pennant race. Chris Von der Ahe was fined $1,500 by the league office for the forfeit, but decided not to send his players out the following day, a Sunday. The Dodgers played their Sunday games in Ridgewood in Queens, even though state laws prohibited Sunday amusements. The Queens County sheriff tacitly allowed the games to continue without interference, but since he was technically violating the law by doing so, he could not send any of his officers to the grounds. With no police presence and a large crowd inflamed by the pennant race and the September 7 game, Von der Ahe feared for the safety of his players. Umpire Fred Goldsmith declared another forfeit in favor of Brooklyn. The last two games of the four-game series, scheduled for September 9 and 10, were rained out. On September 23, a special American Association meeting reversed the September 7 forfeit and awarded the Cardinals a 4-2 victory, but the forfeit of September 8 stood. The Cardinals ended the season with a 90-45 record, two games behind the Dodgers.

Cardinals

09
September

The question of the day: When did the Cardinals begin playing night games during the regular season? The National League allowed its clubs to install lights for night baseball beginning in 1935. Three clubs—the Reds, Cardinals and Cubs—expressed interest in staging night games. The Reds went ahead with the plans, and played the first of seven 1935 night games on May 24 against the Phillies. Cubs owner P. K. Wrigley was intrigued with the notion, but decided against night play. By 1948, the Cubs were the only club in the majors playing day games only. The first night game at Wrigley Field didn't occur until 1988. An enthusiastic proponent of night baseball, Cardinals owner Sam Breadon would have installed lights at Sportsman's Park in 1935 if he owned the ballpark. The Browns held title to the facility, and refused to add lights. The Cards didn't play night games at home until 1940. The Cards did, however, play night exhibition games at Sportsman's Park in 1932. The barnstorming House of David team traveled with a portable lighting system, and the Cardinals played several games against the club at night.

Cardinals

10
September

In a weird game on this date in 1953, the Cardinals were forced to return from the clubhouse to close out a 7-6 win over the Giants at Busch Stadium. With two outs in the top of the ninth, New York runners on first and second, and the score 7-5, Dusty Rhodes grounded to shortstop Solly Hemus, who threw the ball to Red Schoendienst at second for an apparent force out. Umpire Lee Ballanfant signaled out but didn't notice that Schoendienst had dropped the ball. As the Cardinals raced for the clubhouse, the Giants intercepted the umpires, who conferred on the play. They reversed the decision and called the runner safe, which loaded the bases. The Cardinals were called back to the field. After Al Brazle issued a walk to Bobby Hofman, which scored a run, Brazle fielded Daryl Spencer's grounder and threw to first baseman Steve Bilko for the final out.

11
September

At Shea Stadium on this date in 1974, the Cardinals defeated the Mets 4-3 in 25 innings in the second-longest game in major league history. The contest lasted seven hours and four minutes and ended at 3:13 a.m. Among those in attendance were commissioner Bowie Kuhn and his wife. The couple stayed until the conclusion. The Cardinals trailed 3-1 with two out in the ninth when Ken Reitz hit a two-run homer. The two clubs then combined for 15 consecutive scoreless innings. In the 25th, Bake McBride led off with an infield single. When New York pitcher Hank Webb threw wildly on a pickoff attempt, McBride raced to third. First baseman John Milner retrieved the ball in foul territory and threw to catcher Ron Hodges to head off McBride. Hodges dropped the ball allowing McBride to score. St. Louis relievers Mike Garman, Al Hrabosky, Rich Folkers, Ray Bare, Claude Osteen and Sonny Siebert combined for 19 consecutive scoreless innings. Osteen pitched 9⅓ innings, exiting for Siebert in the 23rd with one out and runners on first and second. The two teams combined to use 50 players in the tilt, 26 of them by the Cardinals.

Cardinals

12
September

The question of the day: How close did the Cardinals and Mets come to setting a major league record for the longest game in history on September 11, 1974?

The only longer game in major league history was a 26-inning affair between the Boston Braves and Brooklyn Dodgers on May 1, 1920 in Boston. Another 25-inning game took place later on May 8 and 9, 1984 between the White Sox and Brewers in Chicago. They had played 17 innings on May 8 before umpires suspended the game after 17 innings because of the 1:00 a.m. curfew. The game continued the following evening with eight more innings. The White Sox won 5-4. On September 13, 1974, two nights after playing 25 innings, the Cardinals participated in a 17-inning affair and beat the Phillies 7-3 at Veterans Stadium. There were no runs scored from the fourth through the 16th. The Cards erupted for five runs in the 17th and the Phils countered with one. St. Louis batters drew 16 walks. Philadelphia used a National League record 27 players. The Cardinals put 24 into the box score.

Cardinals

13
September

The question of the day: When did the Mets and Cardinals play another game of 20 or more innings?

The Cardinals and Mets engaged in a 20-inning match on April 17, 2010, at Busch Stadium, with the Mets winning 2-1. There were 19 pitchers in the game, ten of them Cardinals. The first 18 innings were scoreless. Starting pitcher Jamie Garcia allowed only one hit, a sixth-inning single to Angel Pagan, in seven innings on the mound. The Mets didn't collect another hit until the 12th. The nine St. Louis pitchers through the first 18 innings were Garcia, Kyle McClellan, Michael Boggs, Trever Miller, Jason Motte, Dennys Reyes, Blake Hawksworth, Ryan Franklin and Felipe Lopez. It was Lopez's first professional appearance as a pitcher. He started the game at shortstop then moved to third base before taking the mound. Out of position players, Tony La Russa moved Kyle Lohse to left field. Joe Mather, who entered the game as a pinch-hitter in the 10th inning, then played center field and third base, made his first professional pitching debut by hurling the 19th and the 20th. Both teams scored in the 19th before the Mets won it in the 20th. The game lasted six hours and 53 minutes.

14
September

The question of the day: When did Mark McGwire play only the first inning of six games in a row?

On a six-game road trip through Milwaukee and Pittsburgh from September 8 through September 13 in 2000, Mark McGwire played only in the top of the first inning. Still recovering from an injured knee, McGwire wasn't yet ready to play defense and was limited to one at-bat per game. To ensure that McGwire would get a plate appearance and have ample time to warm up the knee, Tony La Russa batted him in either the first or second slot in the batting order. He batted once in the leadoff spot, for the only time in his career as a starter, and hit second in the other five games. McGwire was listed as a second baseman in four games, the left fielder in one, and as the shortstop in another, but he never took the field at any of those positions, or at any other time during his career. In the six games, he hit a home run, was hit by a pitch, and made four outs.

Cardinals

15
September

On this date in 1969, Steve Carlton set a major league record by striking out 19 batters, but the Cardinals lost 4-3 to the Mets at Busch Memorial Stadium. All four New York runs scored on a pair of two-run homers by Ron Swoboda in the fourth and eighth innings. Heading into the contest, the modern (since 1900) major league record for strikeouts in a nine-inning game was 18 by Bob Feller, Sandy Koufax (twice), and Don Wilson. Carlton broke the record by striking out two batters in the eighth inning and three in the ninth. During the ninth, he also broke the Cardinals' team record of 17 set by Dizzy Dean in 1933 and Bob Gibson in the 1968 World Series. Carlton later admitted that he was going for a strikeout while facing every hitter in the late innings and that the strategy cost him the game. Carlton walked two, allowed nine hits, and threw 152 pitches. His major league record was tied by Tom Seaver in 1970 and Nolan Ryan in 1974 before Roger Clemens struck out 20 batters in 1986. Clemens also fanned 20 in 1996 and Kerry Wood matched it in 1998. Randy Johnson fanned 20 in the first nine innings of an 11-inning game in 2001. Carlton's 19 strikeouts on September 15, 1969, are still the Cardinals team record.

Cardinals

16
September

The Cardinals took over first place on this date in 1930 with a dramatic, ten-inning 1-0 victory over the Dodgers at Ebbets Field. Wild Bill Hallahan of St. Louis and Dazzy Vance of Brooklyn both pitched complete games. Pitching with a sore finger on his right (non-pitching) hand he injured when he caught it in the door of a cab, Hallahan retired the first 20 batters to face him before Babe Herman reached on an error when Hallahan fumbled a grounder. The first Brooklyn hit was a single by Harvey Hendrick with one out in the eighth. In the tenth, St. Louis pinch-hitter Andy High hit a double. Hallahan sacrificed High to second with two strikes on him, and Taylor Douthit singled for the 1-0 lead. In the bottom of the inning, the Dodgers loaded the bases, but a double play ended the contest. The twin killing started when shortstop Sparky Adams barehanded a sizzling grounder by Al Lopez. The victory put the Cards one percentage point ahead of the Dodgers and 1½ games up on the Cubs. The season ended on September 28 with the Cardinals leading the second-place Cubs by two games.

Cardinals

17
September

On this date in 1920, the Cardinals launched 12 straight hits in the fourth and fifth innings to set a major league record for most consecutive hits, during a 9-4 win over the Braves in Boston. With one out in the fourth, the Cards got ten hits in succession and scored eight runs. The last two men in the inning were thrown out trying to take an extra base. Milt Stock was out attempting to make it to second base on a single, and Austin McHenry was retired trying to stretch a double into a triple. Doc Lavan opened the fifth with a double and Cliff Heathcote followed with a single before Verne Clemons popped out to shortstop Rabbit Maranville to end the streak. McHenry, Lavan and Heathcote each collected two of the 12 consecutive hits. The others were picked up by Clemons, Bill Doak, Mike Knode, Jack Fournier, Milt Stock and Rogers Hornsby. Boston pitcher Mule Watson gave up the first five hits, George McQuillan the next five, and Leo Townsend the final two.

18
September

On this date in 1968, a no-hitter was pitched for the second game in a row in a series between the Cardinals and Giants at Candlestick Park. In a night game on September 17, San Francisco's Gaylord Perry no-hit the Cardinals for a 1-0 win. Curt Flood struck out for the final out of the game. Bob Gibson was the losing pitcher. The following afternoon, Ray Washburn turned the tables by no-hitting the Giants for a 2-0 Cardinals victory. In the ninth, Ron Hunt hit a sharp grounder to Phil Gagliano at second base for the first out. Willie Mays followed with a grounder to Mike Shannon for out number two. Willie McCovey hit a fly ball to Curt Flood in center for the final out. Washburn walked five and struck out eight. It was the first time a no-hitter had been pitched in consecutive games involving the same two teams. It has happened once since then. On April 30, 1969, Jim Maloney of the Reds threw a no-hitter against the Astros at Crosley Field, and the following night, Don Wilson of Houston no-hit Cincinnati.

Cardinals

19
September

The question of the day. How many managers led the Cardinals to NL pennants between 1926 and 1946?

The Cardinals won nine NL pennants from 1926 through 1946 despite changing managers frequently. The managers during that period were Rogers Hornsby (1925–26), Bob O'Farrell (1927), Bill McKechnie (1928), Billy Southworth (1929), McKechnie again (1929), Gabby Street (1930–33), Frankie Frisch (1934–38), Mike Gonzalez (1938), Ray Blades (1939–40), Gonzalez for a second time (1940), Southworth once more (1940–45) and Eddie Dyer (1946–50). The pennants were won by Hornsby (1926), McKechnie (1928), Street (1930 and 1931), Frisch (1934), Southworth (1942, 1943 and 1944) and Dyer (1946). Since 1946, NL pennants have been won by managers Johnny Keane (1964), Red Schoendienst (1967 and 1968), Whitey Herzog (1982, 1985 and 1987) and Tony La Russa (2004 and 2006). World championships have been claimed by Hornsby (1926), Street (1931), Frisch (1934), Southworth (1942 and 1944), Dyer (1946), Keane (1964), Schoendienst (1967), Herzog (1982) and La Russa (2006).

Cardinals

20
September

On this date in 1928, George Harper became the first Cardinal batter to collect three homers in a game since 1894, during an 8-5 victory over the Giants in the first game of a doubleheader at the Polo Grounds. Harper hit a solo homer off Rube Benton in the second inning, a three-run shot off Benton in the sixth, and another solo home run against Jack Scott in the eighth. Harper batted in the ninth with the bases loaded, but was called out on strikes. Harper was so incensed over the call by umpire Cy Rigler that he had to be dragged to the dugout by teammate Rabbit Maranville. New York won the second game 7-4. The twin bill was played during a tight pennant race between the Cardinals and Giants. The day ended as it started with the Cardinals holding a two-game advantage over the Giants. The Cards clinched the pennant nine days later on the second-to-last day of the regular season.

Cardinals

21
September

On this date in 1883, a crowd of 10,000 turned out amid swirling winds at Sportsman's Park for the American Association pennant show-down between the Cardinals and the Philadelphia Athletics. Among those in attendance were Missouri Governor Thomas Crittenden and Congressman John O'Neill. Despite the enthusiastic throng, the Cardinals lost 13-11 in the first game of a three-game series. St. Louis committed 12 errors, five of them by third baseman Arlie Latham, who had so much difficulty field-ing the hot corner that manager Charlie Comiskey switched him with catcher Pat Deasley in the eighth inning despite the fact that Latham hadn't caught a game all year. Latham allowed three passed balls in one inning as a backstop, which helped Philadelphia score four runs to increase its lead to 13-8. Amazingly, the Athletics were even worse defensively, making 16 errors during the afternoon. The win gave Philadelphia a 3½-game lead. The Cardinals finished the season one game behind the Athletics. Latham is the oldest major leaguer ever to steal a base—as a 49-year-old player coach. He lived to be 92.

Cardinals

22
September

The question of the day: Which Cardinals players left the club to play in Mexico?

Pitchers Max Lanier and Fred Martin and infielder Lou Klein accepted offers to play in the Mexican League on May 23, 1946. The Mexican League was controlled by the five Pasquel brothers, who belonged to one of Mexico's richest and most politically powerful families. Jorge Pasquel was the one determined to upgrade Mexican baseball and create a third major league by attracting big leaguers with offers of much higher salaries than they were being paid in the States. In all, the brothers persuaded 18 players to take their offer, most notably Mickey Owen of the Dodgers and Sal Maglie of the Giants. Lanier was the biggest loss for the Cardinals. He had a record of 6-0 when he left for Mexico and appeared to be on the verge of developing into a staff ace. All of those who jumped to Mexico were suspended by commissioner Happy Chandler for five years.

Cardinals

23
September

The question of the day: How did Cardinals owner Sam Breadon try to prevent further defections to Mexico?

In June 1946, Breadon traveled to Mexico to talk to Jorge Pasquel, who had also made overtures to Cardinals players Stan Musial, Marty Marion, Enos Slaughter, Whitey Kurowski and Terry Moore. The Cards were prime targets of the Pasquel brothers because of the talent on the roster and Breadon's stinginess. Musial had been offered $75,000 and a five-year contract calling for $125,000 to play in Mexico at a time when he was making $13,500. Breadon received a promise from Pasquel that he wouldn't pursue any more Cardinals. The Mexican League proved to be a failure, and most of the players who went there soon regretted the decision. Much of the promised money never materialized, and living and playing conditions were often primitive when compared to major league standards. Commissioner Happy Chandler lifted the five-year suspensions imposed in 1946 and reinstated the players in 1949. At that time, Max Lanier, Fred Martin and Lou Klein returned to the Cardinals.

Cardinals

24 September

On this date in 1926, the Cardinals clinched their first National League pennant with a 6-4 win over the Giants in New York. Bill Terry hit a three-run homer off Flint Rhem in the first inning, but the Cards rebounded with five runs in the second. Some 50 loudspeakers were set up in the downtown business area carrying the radio broadcast of the Cardinals-Giants game. Thousands gathered on the streets to hear the play-by-play from New York. Once the last out was made, the pent-up feeling of Cardinals fans, who hadn't celebrated a pennant since the club won the American Association title in 1888, erupted in jubilation. According to a report in *The Sporting News*, "Great cheers went up from these many assemblages, and immediately a demonstration was on. Factory whistles shrieked, automobilists tooted their horns, trucks went about with cutouts open and the drivers backfiring their engines, impromptu bands and parades were organized and howling thousands surged through the streets, tying up traffic in general. From office buildings, great wads of paper, ticker tape and confetti were released, falling like the snow of a Dakota blizzard on the pavement below."

Cardinals

25
September

On this date in 1956, the Cardinals pulled off an unusual triple play during a 5-1 win over the Cubs at Wrigley Field. The bases were loaded in the Chicago fifth, with Dave Hillman on first, Hobie Landrith on second, and Gene Baker on third when Solly Drake drilled a line drive to Stan Musial at first base. Musial appeared to have trapped the ball but actually caught it at ankle level. In the ensuing confusion, Musial threw to shortstop Dick Schofield to double Landrith at second, but Schofield's return throw to second baseman Don Blasingame, covering first, was too late to catch Hillman off the bag. Blasingame flipped the ball to pitcher Lindy McDaniel, who heard manager Fred Hutchinson's shouts from the dugout and fired across the diamond to triple Baker, who had tried to run home on the play and was tagged out by third baseman Ken Boyer in a rundown.

Cardinals

26
September

On this date in 1983, Bob Forsch pitched his second career no-hitter, defeating the Expos 3-0 at Busch Stadium. Forsch threw 96 pitches, retired the last 22 batters to face him, walked none and struck out six. The only two Montreal base runners were Gary Carter, who was hit by a pitch, and Chris Speier, who reached on an error by third baseman Ken Oberkfell. Both occurred in the second inning. Terry Crowley led off the ninth and struck out looking at a 2-2 pitch. Umpires ejected Crowley for arguing the call. Terry Francona followed with a routine fly ball to right fielder Danny Green. Manny Trillo made the final out on a grounder to Oberkfell. The victory was Forsch's first as a starter since July 28. He had been relegated to the bullpen for much of August and September because of ineffectiveness. Forsch is the only Cardinal to pitch two no-hitters, and he pitched the only two no-hitters of nine innings or more in the 40-year history of the second Busch Stadium. He threw his first no-hitter on April 16, 1978. Oddly, Forsch pitched the no-hitters in two of the worst seasons of his career. He was 11-17 in 1978 and 10-12 in 1983. He posted a lifetime record of 168-136.

Cardinals

27
September

On this date in 1983, the Cardinals turned an unusual triple play during a 10-4 loss to the Expos at Busch Stadium. With the bases loaded in the fourth inning, Andre Dawson hit a hard shot to second baseman Jeff Doyle, who threw to shortstop Ozzie Smith for the force at second. Smith's toss to first baseman Jim Adduci got Dawson for the second out. Terry Francona, the runner at second, believed that Doyle had caught the ball on the fly and thought he was retired on the throw to Smith. Francona wandered away from the base and was called out after he had gone into the dugout. It was the 11th big league game for Doyle and just the seventh for Adduci. Doyle played in only 13 contests during his career. Adduci appeared in only ten games as a member of the Cardinals, and batted .050 in 20 at-bats.

Cardinals

28
September

During a 3-0 loss to the Cubs at Sportsman's Park on this date in 1952, Stan Musial made the only pitching appearance of his career. It was the last game of the season, and Musial went into the game with a .336 to .326 lead over Chicago outfielder Frank Baumholtz in the race for the batting title. With one out in the first inning, Musial came in from his center field position to pitch to Baumholtz, while pitcher Harvey Haddix went to the outfield. A left-handed batter, Baumholtz switched to the right side and hit a weak grounder to third baseman Solly Hemus, who fumbled the ball for an error. Musial returned to the outfield and won the batting championship by going one-for-three while Baumholtz was one-for-four. Musial finished the year at .336 while Baumholtz ended with a .325 average.

29
September

On this date in 1963, Stan Musial played the last of his 3,206 major league games, a 3-2 win in 14 innings over the Reds at Busch Stadium. During batting practice, many Reds asked Musial to pose with them for photographs and asked for his autograph. Among them was rookie second baseman Pete Rose, who was five months old when Musial made his major league debut and would later break Musial's National League career record for hits in 1981. Rose shook Musial's hand and wished him well. Musial was presented with a framed six-foot-by-four-foot painting of a statue that later adorned the new Busch Stadium, which opened downtown in 1966. He was also given a diamond ring with the number 6. Two Cub scouts presented Musial with a neckerchief, which remained around his neck for the duration of the program. Afterward, he was driven around the stands in a convertible accompanied by his family and waved to the fans. In Musial's first plate appearance, Cincinnati pitcher Jim Maloney caught him looking at strike three. In the fourth inning, Musial smashed a single just past Rose. Two innings later, Musial smashed another single to right. Gary Kolb went in as a pinch-runner, and Musial received a tumultuous standing ovation as he trotted off the field for the last time as a player.

Cardinals

30
September

On this date in 1883, the Cardinals closed out the season with a 6-3 win against Pittsburgh in St. Louis. The Cardinals ended the year one game behind the Philadelphia Athletics and took out their frustration over losing the pennant on third baseman Arlie Latham, who they blamed for finishing second instead of first. The St. Louis players were angry because Latham had an extraordinary talent for badgering the opposition and the umpires with his derisive wit, and he often directed his sarcasm at teammates. Latham's ability to use his mouth as a weapon earned him the nickname "The Freshest Man on Earth." At the end of the September 30 game, Cardinals players trapped Latham in the clubhouse, and the entire roster fought him one by one. As soon as Latham fended off one teammate, another took his place. A few knocked Latham out cold, but, once revived, he had to fight the next player in line.

Cardinals

October

Cardinals

**01
October**

During a 2-1 loss to the Cubs on this date in 1939, catcher Don Padgett lost a chance to finish the season with a batting average of .400. Padgett entered the final game of the year with an average of .399 in 253 at-bats. Pinch-hitting in the eighth inning, Padgett lined a clean single up the middle, but upon reaching first base, learned that the first-base umpire had called time a split second before the pitch because a ball rolled loose in the bullpen. Padgett returned to the plate and drew a walk in what proved to be his last plate appearance of the season with an average of .39914. Had the hit stood, his season batting average would have been .402. Padgett had an unusual career, because he was converted from an outfielder to a catcher in 1938 in his second season in the majors at a time when he was 26 years old and a string of injuries hit the Cardinals catchers. Padgett played in 251 games as a catcher and 246 in the outfield during his big league career. He played in his final game in the majors in 1948 and finished with a batting average of .288.

Cardinals

02
October

On this date in 1968, the Cardinals won the first game of the World Series 4-0 over the Tigers 54,692 at Busch Memorial Stadium. Bob Gibson set a World Series record with 17 strikeouts. The Cards scored three runs in the fourth inning and added an insurance run on a homer by Lou Brock in the seventh. The contest was a much-anticipated match-up of Gibson and Denny McLain, two pitchers who won the Most Valuable Player Award in 1968. McLain had a record of 31-6 to become baseball's only 30-game winner since Dizzy Dean in 1934. (No one has won more than 27 games in a season since then.) Gibson was 22-9 with a 1.12 ERA in 1968. In the World Series opener, Gibson was almost untouchable, allowing only five hits. He struck out two batters in the first inning, three in the second, two in the third, one in the fourth, one in the fifth, two in the sixth, two in the seventh, one in the eighth and three in the ninth. Gibson headed into the ninth with 14 strikeouts, one shy of the World Series record set by Sandy Koufax of the Dodgers in 1963. After allowing a single to Mickey Stanley, Gibson fanned Al Kaline, Norm Cash and Willie Horton in succession.

Cardinals

03
October

On this date in 1926, the Cardinals won game two of the World Series with a 6-2 victory over the Yankees in New York. Grover Alexander allowed two runs in the second inning to fall behind 2-0, but shutout the Yankees the rest of the way and retired the last 21 batters to face him. He fanned ten batters in the game. The Cards tied the score 2-2 in the third on a single by Jim Bottomley. A three-run homer by Billy Southworth in the seventh broke the deadlock. Tommy Thevenow, who hit only two regular season homers in 4,164 at-bats during his career, hit an inside-the-park home run in the ninth inning. Thevenow hit a drive to the farthest corner of right field. Babe Ruth gave chase, hesitated just before arriving to avoid a collision with the concrete wall, then hit the wall anyway. By the time Ruth found the ball, Thevenow had rounded the bases. Thevenow holds the all-time major league record for most consecutive at-bats without a home run during the regular season with 3,347 from September 24, 1926, through the end of his career on October 2, 1938. During that span, he played for the Cardinals, Pirates, Reds and Braves.

Cardinals

04
October

On the last day of the regular season on this date in 1964, the Cardinals clinched the National League pennant with an 11-5 win over the Mets at Busch Stadium. As recently as September 20, the Cards were tied for second place with the Reds and were 6½ games behind the first-place Phillies. St. Louis came into the day tied for first place with the Reds and one game ahead of the Phillies. The Cards took a 5-3 lead with three runs in the fifth. Bob Gibson was the winning pitcher with four innings of relief just two days after pitching a complete game. (He would pitch three more complete games, two of them wins and one of 10 innings, during the World Series on October 8, 12 and 15). Barney Schultz earned the save, his fifth in the Cards' last 12 games, a period in which he pitched 11 scoreless innings. The Reds were eliminated with a 10-0 loss to Philadelphia in Cincinnati.

Cardinals

05
October

On this date in 1942, the Cardinals won the World Series over the Yankees in New York. A homer by Enos Slaughter in the fourth inning tied the score 1-1. Walker Cooper's sacrifice fly in the sixth deadlocked the contest at 2-2. The Cardinals won the tilt in the ninth when Whitey Kurowski hit a two-run home run just inside the left field foul pole with one out facing Red Ruffing. Johnny Beazley pitched the complete game win. To reach the World Series, the Cardinals had to win an exciting pennant race against the Brooklyn Dodgers. The Redbirds trailed the Dodgers by ten games on August 5, and won 43 of their final 51 games to take the NL pennant by two games. The Cards were 106-48 during the regular season in 1942 before compiling a 4-1 mark in the World Series. The 106 wins are the most in Cardinals history and the most of any National League club between the 1909 Pirates and the 1975 Reds. No NL team since 1942 has a better winning percentage than the .688 mark recorded by the Cards that year. Despite the remarkable season, the Cardinals were the underdog heading into the World Series. The Yankees were 103-51 in 1942 and had won the world championship in five of the previous six seasons in 1936, 1937, 1938, 1939 and 1941.

Cardinals

06
October

On this date in 1943, the Cardinals defeated the Yankees 4-3 in game two of the World Series in New York behind a complete game by Mort Cooper. Marty Marion started the scoring with a 320-foot home run down the left field line to lead off the third inning. The Cards added three more runs in the fourth, two of them on a homer by Ray Sanders. St. Louis led 4-1 heading into the ninth when the Yankees scored twice. On the final out, Joe Gordon fouled out to catcher Walker Cooper, who was Mort's brother. In the morning, Mort and Walker received word that their father had passed away in Independence, Missouri. After mulling it over, the Cooper brothers decided their dad would have wanted them to play in the game. The two put aside their grief long enough to beat the Yankees, with Walker calling the signals for Mort's complete game. At the plate, Walker was one-for-three with a sacrifice. After the game, Mort and Walker boarded a train to attend their father's funeral. The Yankees won the final three games of the 1943 World Series to defeat the Cardinals four games to one.

Cardinals

07
October

On this date in 1885, the city of St. Louis staged a nighttime parade and a sumptuous banquet at Schnaider's Beer Garden to honor the 1885 American Association champion Cardinals. An estimated 250,000 people lined the streets. The procession through the main thoroughfares of the city was led by mounted police, the United States Cavalry band, and the state militia. Local amateur clubs marched during the festivities, as did the Cincinnati Reds and New York Giants. A pretty young woman sat atop a Sportsman's Park float that contained pictures of Cardinal players. Chris Von der Ahe rode behind the float in a carriage with his guests. A local social club provided a wagonload of ammunition and fire works, and many in the crowd came equipped with pyrotechnics of their own, including live bombs, torches, Roman candles and pinwheels. Shotgun blasts from upper-story windows punctuated the night air. Not surprisingly, the event was marred by a number of injuries. United States Vice-President Thomas Hendricks was in St. Louis to attend an agricultural fair. Under the mistaken notion that the parade was being held to welcome him, Hendricks began to make a speech from the balcony of his room at the Southern Hotel, thanking the citizens of St. Louis for their hospitality.

Cardinals

08
October

On this date in 2009, the Dodgers scored two runs in the ninth inning to stun the Cardinals 3-2 in Los Angeles in game two of the Division Series. Matt Holliday homered in the second to give the Cardinals a 1-0 lead. Adam Wainwright retired the first 11 batters to face him before Andre Ethier homered in the fourth. Mark DeRosa put St. Louis into the lead with an RBI-double in the seventh. With Ryan Franklin on the mound, the Cards still had a 2-1 lead with two out in the ninth and no one on base. But Holliday, playing left field, dropped a line drive off the bat of James Loney for an error on what should have been the final out. Franklin walked Casey Blake on a 3-2 pitch and gave up a single to Rafael Belliard to tie the score 2-2. A passed ball advanced both runners and a walk to Russell Martin loaded the bases. Mark Loretta drove in the winning run with a single. The Dodgers completed the sweep of the Cardinals two nights later with a 5-1 triumph at Busch Stadium.

Cardinals

09
October

On this date in 1968, the Tigers forced a game seven by beating the Cardinals 13-1 before 54,692 at Busch Memorial Stadium. Detroit blew the game wide open with ten runs in the third inning off Ray Washburn, Larry Jaster and Ron Willis. Jim Northrup hit a grand slam. Tigers' manager Mayo Smith gambled by pitching Denny McLain on two days' rest, and McLain responded with a complete game. Fewer than 10,000 fans were in the stands at the finish as the rout and a 45-minute rain delay in the eighth sent most of the crowd scurrying for home. Two days earlier, in game five in Detroit, the Cardinals held a 3-0 lead in the first inning and still held a 3-2 advantage in the seventh. Just nine outs from the world championship, the Cardinals allowed three runs to lose 5-3. In game seven on October 10, Mickey Lolich outdueled Bob Gibson to give the Tigers a 4-1 win. Gibson retired 20 of the first 21 batters to face him and the score was 0-0 when the Tigers scored three runs in the top of the seventh.

Cardinals

10
October

On this date in 1926, the Cardinals claimed their first modern world championship with a 3-2 win over the Yankees in game seven of the World Series at Yankee Stadium. Jesse Haines of the Cards and Waite Hoyt of the Yanks, both future Hall of Famers, were the starting pitchers in the decisive match, which was played in a steady drizzle. Babe Ruth homered off Haines in the third for a 1-0 lead. But shoddy Yankee fielding in the fourth gave the Cards a 3-1 lead. Tommy Thevenow broke the 1-1 tie with a two-run single. After getting a run back in the sixth to make the score 3-2, the Yanks loaded the bases in the seventh against Haines, who had worn a blister on his index finger. Player-manager Rogers Hornsby held a long conference on the mound with catcher Bob O'Farrell and the rest of the infield and decided to bring 39-year-old Grover Alexander into the game. Alexander had not only pitched a complete game victory the day before, beating the Yankees 10-2, but according to legend, celebrated far into the evening, believing he wouldn't pitch again. According to many teammates, Alexander reported to the ballpark severely hung over and was sleeping in the bullpen when summoned by Hornsby.

Cardinals

11
October

The question of the day: What happened after Grover Alexander entered game seven of the 1926 World Series with the bases loaded and two out in the seventh inning holding a 3-2 lead?

The first batter Alexander faced was Tony Lazzeri. On a 1-1 pitch, Lazzeri drilled a long foul. Alexander struck him out on the next pitch. In the eighth, Alexander set down the Yankees in order. In the ninth, he retired Earle Combs and Mark Koenig, and then walked Babe Ruth. With Bob Meusel at the plate, Ruth impulsively tried to steal second. Catcher Bob O'Farrell gunned the ball to second baseman Rogers Hornsby, who slapped the tag on the Babe in plenty of time to end the game and make the Cards the champs. A boisterous celebration erupted on the streets of St. Louis. Property damage was extensive and two teenagers were killed when struck by automobiles. Approximately 80 people were treated at local hospitals for injuries.

Cardinals

12
October

Heading into the day trailing the Dodgers two games to none in the NLCS, the Cardinals emerged with a 4-2 victory before 53,708 at Busch Stadium on this date in 1985. The Cards scored two runs in each of the first two innings, two by Vince Coleman. He unnerved the Dodgers by leading off the first with a single and immediately stealing second. Dodger pitcher Bob Welch tried to pick Coleman off second, but threw the ball into center field, and Coleman sped all the way home. In the second, Coleman walked and moved to third on an errant pickoff attempt by catcher Mike Scioscia. Tom Herr provided the second run of the inning with a homer. Danny Cox was the winning pitcher, and third baseman Terry Pendleton made two dazzling defensive plays. Game three of the NLCS proved to be Coleman's last appearance in the 1985 postseason. In a freak accident, the fastest man in baseball was disabled by Busch Stadium's slow-moving automatic tarpaulin. While performing stretching exercises just prior to game four on October 13, the tarp, which weighed nearly a ton, rolled over Coleman's left leg up to his thigh. He was trapped for 30 seconds before the grounds crew could roll back the tarp. Coleman was removed from the field on a stretcher and was diagnosed with a bone chip near his left knee.

Cardinals

13
October

On this date in 1987, the Cardinals staved off elimination in the NLCS by beating the Giants 1-0 in game six before 53,331 at Busch Stadium. John Tudor (7⅓ innings), Todd Worrell (one inning) and Ken Dayley (two-third of an inning) combined on the shutout. Dave Dravecky, who two-hit the Cards in game two, was the losing pitcher. The lone run of the game scored in the second inning. Tony Pena led off with a triple that Giants right fielder Candy Maldonado lost in the lights. One out later, Jose Oquendo hit a sacrifice fly. Worrell started the ninth with a strikeout against Will Clark, but Whitey Herzog brought in Dayley to face left-handed Harry Spilman and switch-hitter Jose Uribe. Worrell was moved to right field in case he was needed for one more out. He wasn't. Dayley retired Chris Speier, who batted for Spilman, and Uribe to seal the victory. The next day, the Cards advanced to the World Series by beating the Giants 6-0 before 55,331 in St. Louis. Danny Cox pitched the shutout. Oquendo, who entered the game with two career homers in 903 regular season at-bats, hit a 3-2 pitch from Atlee Hammaker over the wall in the second inning with two runners on base. The Cardinals' pitching staff closed out the 1987 NLCS with 22 consecutive scoreless innings.

Cardinals

14
October

On this date in 1985, the Cardinals moved within one victory of the NL pennant when Ozzie Smith hit a walkoff homer off Tom Nieden-fuer with one out in the ninth inning to defeat the Dodgers 3-2 at Busch Stadium. The slick-fielding shortstop shocked the nationwide television audi-ence and those at the ballpark by lashing a line drive on a 1-2 pitch down the right field line for a home run. Smith leaped for joy when he saw the ball hit the cement pillar above the wall and literally danced around the bases. On the radio, Jack Buck immortalized the moment with his famous call: "Smith corks one right down the line. It may go! Go crazy, folks! Go crazy! It's a home run, and the Cardinals have won the game 3-2 on a home run by the Wizard!" Entering the game, Smith had 13 career homers in 4,225 at-bats and 50 postseason at-bats. The switch-hitter had never hit a homer from the left side of the plate as a major leaguer in more than 3,000 at-bats. During the 1986 and 1987 seasons, Smith batted 1,114 times without a single homer. His next homer didn't occur until 1988 after a stretch of 1,327 homerless at-bats. Smith's first regular season home run while batting left-handed was on June 12, 1988, in his 4,612th at-bat from that side of the plate. Over his career, Smith had five regular season homers from the left side in 6,280 at-bats.

15
October

On this date in 1964, the Cardinals claimed the world championship with a 7-5 win over the Yankees before 30,346 at Busch Stadium. The starting pitchers were Bob Gibson and Mel Stottlemyre, each pitching on two days' rest. The Cards took a 3-0 lead with three runs in the fourth inning. One of the runs scored on a double steal with Tim McCarver swiping home and Mike Shannon taking second. Three more followed in the fifth, the first on a solo homer by Lou Brock. With Gibson on the mound, a 6-0 lead seemed secure, but the Yankees went down fighting. Mickey Mantle hit a three-run homer in the sixth. Ken Boyer homered in the seventh to give the Cardinals a 7-3 lead, and he gave his brother Clete, the Yankees' third baseman, a playful pat on the back rounding third on his home run trot. Clete returned the gesture when he kept the Yankees in the game with a homer in the ninth. Phil Linz followed with a two-out homer to make the score 7-5. Gibson closed out the game, however, by inducing Bobby Richardson, who had 13 hits in the Series, to pop out to second baseman Julian Javier. The Boyers are the only pair of brothers to each hit a home run in the same World Series. McCarver is the only catcher to steal home in a World Series.

Cardinals

16
October

On this date in 1985, Jack Clark provided the heroics with a ninth-inning homer to lift the Cardinals to the NL pennant with a 7-5 win over the Dodgers in Los Angeles. The Cards trailed 4-1 heading into the seventh. Willie McGee narrowed the gap with a two-run single off Orel Hershiser. Tom Niedenfuer replaced Hershiser, and the first batter he faced was Ozzie Smith, who had touched the reliever for a homer on the last pitch of game five two days earlier. Smith responded with a triple to score McGee and tie the contest at 4-4. The Dodgers took the lead in the eighth, however, when Mike Marshall homered off Todd Worrell. Niedenfuer was still on the mound in the ninth. Willie McGee singled and stole second. Smith walked, and both he and McGee moved up a base on Tom Herr's groundout. With first base open, Dodger manager Tommy Lasorda elected to pitch to Clark. On the first pitch from Niedenfuer, Clark belted a 450-foot home run into the left field bleachers to give the Cards a 7-5 lead. Ken Dayley retired all three batters he faced in the ninth, two on strikeouts, to give the Cards the win.

Cardinals

17
October

On this date in 2005, the Cardinals were one strike away from a season-ending loss before a three-run, ninth-inning rally beat the Astros 5-4 in game five of the NLCS in Houston. The Cards took a 2-1 lead in the fourth when Mark Grudzielanek flared a single into the outfield with the bases loaded and two out. Houston took the lead back when Lance Berkman sliced a three-run homer into the Crawford boxes off Chris Carpenter in the seventh. The Cards still trailed 4-2 entering the ninth when Brad Lidge took the mound for the third night in a row. Lidge retired the first two batters before David Eckstein took his place in the batter's box with the crowd at Minute Maid Park anticipating a pennant celebration. The count was 1-2 when Eckstein singled through the hole between short and third. Jim Edmonds walked on five pitches. Then Albert Pujols put the Cardinals ahead with a 412-foot, three-run homer that cleared the train tracks above the left field wall for one of the most dramatic blasts in postseason history. Jason Isringhausen pitched a scoreless ninth to preserve the victory. The euphoria over Pujols's home run lasted only 48 hours, however, as the Astros won game six 5-1 two nights later in St. Louis to take the series four games to two.

Cardinals

18
October

Today's trivia: What was "Slaughter's Mad Dash?"

Enos Slaughter's "mad dash" around the bases provided the winning run in a 4-3 decision over the Red Sox in game seven of the 1946 World Series, played at Sportsman's Park on October 15. St. Louis starting pitcher Murry Dickson took a 3-1 lead into the eighth, but the Red Sox scored two runs. Dickson put two runners on base on a single and a double and was replaced by Harry Brecheen, who surrendered a two-run double to Dom DiMaggio before recording the final out. DiMaggio twisted his ankle on the hit and was replaced in center field by Leon Culberson. In the bottom of the eighth, facing Bob Klinger, Slaughter led off with a single. After Whitey Kurowski and Del Rice were retired, Harry Walker drilled a pitch to left-center. Culberson fielded the ball and threw to shortstop Johnny Pesky. Slaughter got a terrific jump from first base, rounded third, and headed for home. When Pesky turned with the ball in his hand, he was stunned to see Slaughter steaming toward the plate. Pesky hesitated for a split second and put little on the throw. Slaughter was safe, which gave St. Louis a 4-3 lead. Brecheen nailed down the victory in the ninth.

Cardinals

19
October

The question of the day: Could Johnny Pesky have thrown out Enos Slaughter in game seven of the 1946 World Series if he had not hesitated before throwing to home plate?

Whether or not Pesky could have thrown out Slaughter on the play, which has gone into history as "Slaughter's Mad Dash," is a subject baseball fans have debated endlessly. Game film shows that Slaughter had just rounded third when Pesky caught the ball in short left field. Pesky was about 120 feet from home plate and Slaughter was about 70 to 80 feet from home and running at top speed. Pesky turned, and his body language showed surprise that Slaughter was heading home. Pesky hesitated for only a fraction of a second, but even that short time gave the speedy Slaughter an extra 15 feet or so. More important-ly, Pesky appeared to drop his glove slightly, which took him out of position to make a strong throw. Even so, it's likely that it would have taken an almost perfect throw from Pesky and a clean catch and quick tag from catcher Roy Partee to nail Slaughter.

Cardinals

20
October

On this date in 1982, the Cardinals claimed their first world championship since 1967 with a 6-3 win over the Brewers in game seven, played before 53,723 at Busch Memorial Stadium. The Brewers led 3-1 heading into the bottom of the sixth inning and were 12 outs from winning the Series when the Cards scored three runs. St. Louis loaded the bases, and Keith Hernandez stepped to the plate on his 29th birthday facing Milwaukee reliever Bob McClure. Hernandez and McClure grew up 100 feet from each other in San Francisco and played ball together as kids. Hernandez won the battle over his boyhood chum by driving in two runs on a single to tie the score, and he crossed the plate with the go-ahead run on a single by George Hendrick. The Cardinals added two insurance runs in the eighth. Pitching in pain, Joaquin Andujar was the winning pitcher. Five days earlier, Andujar had been removed from game three in the seventh inning when he took a line drive off his kneecap. Bruce Sutter nailed down the save by retiring all six batters he faced. He got the last out on a swinging strikeout by Gorman Thomas.

Cardinals

21
October

On this date in 2004, the Cardinals earned their first trip to the World Series since 1987 with a 5-2 win over the Astros in game seven of the NLCS before 52,140 at Busch Stadium. The Cards headed into game six two days earlier trailing three games to two and won 6-4 in 12 innings. Houston scored in the top of the first, but Albert Pujols put the Cards back in it with a two-run homer in the bottom half. After the Astros tied the score in the third, the Redbirds added two more in their half to lead 4-2. The Astros weren't finished, however, and added runs in the fourth and another in the ninth as Jason Isringhausen blew a save opportunity for the second game in a row. It remained 4-4 until the 12th when Jim Edmonds hit a two-out, two-run, walkoff homer. In game seven, Craig Biggio led off the first inning with a homer off Jeff Suppan, and Houston was still ahead after 5½ innings. The game stayed close in large part because of a sensational diving catch by Edmonds in center field. The Cards took the lead with three runs in the sixth off Roger Clemens. All three runs scored with two outs. Albert Pujols drove in the tying run and scored on a homer by Scott Rolen. The Cards added an insurance run in the eighth.

Cardinals

22
October

On this date in 1912, Cardinals owner Helene Britton fired Roger Bresnahan as manager and replaced him with Miller Huggins. Bresnahan took over the Cardinals after a 49-105 record in 1908 and turned the club into a winner by 1911 when the Cards were 75-74. He was rewarded with a five-year contract calling for $10,000 a year plus ten per cent of the profits. Things turned sour almost immediately after the 1912 season began, however, when the Cards lost 16 of their first 21 games on the way to a 63-90 record. Britton offered Bresnahan a few suggestions on how to improve the club, and in a profanity-filled response, the St. Louis skipper said that no woman was going to tell him what to do. The two argued all season. Bresnahan also wanted to purchase the Cardinals, and Britton refused to listen to any offer to sell. In August, Bresnahan tried to trade Huggins, who was Britton's favorite player, to the Reds. She blocked the deal. Bresnahan had the support of the majority of the fans, players, and reporters who covered the club, however, and his dismissal was not a popular move. In January 1913, the Cubs signed Bresnahan as a catcher and he managed the Chicago team in 1915. Meanwhile, Bresnahan took the Cardinals to court when the club refused to pay the final four years of his five-year contract. He received $20,000 in a settlement.

23
October

On this date in 1995, the Cardinals hired Tony La Russa as manager. La Russa hit only .199 without a single home run in 132 games as a player over six big league seasons. He made his major league debut at 18 with the Kansas City Athletics in 1963, and throughout his playing career, he continued his education. He attended the University of Tampa and the University of South Florida during the offseason and obtained a degree in industrial engineering. He attended law school at Florida State University, graduated in 1978, and passed the bar in 1979. Baseball took priority, however, and he received his first major league managing job with the White Sox in 1979. In 1983, the Sox won the Western Division title with a record of 99-63. The .611 winning percentage was the best of any White Sox team since 1920. It wasn't matched again until 2005. By 1986, however, La Russa was fired after a series of disagreements with general manager Ken Harrelson. A month later, he accepted a job as manager of the Athletics. He led the Oakland club to the World Series in 1988, 1989 and 1990, winning a world championship in 1989. By 1995, the A's had fallen into last place, and Cardinals general manager Walt Jocketty, who had worked with La Russa in Oakland, was able to lure him to St. Louis.

24
October

Today's trivia: How does La Russa rank among the greatest managers of all-time?

Heading into the 2011 season, La Russa ranked third all-time in regular season victories with 2,638. Number one is Connie Mack, who won 3,731 games with the Pittsburgh Pirates (1894–96) and Philadelphia Athletics (1901–50). Mack's victory total is somewhat tainted, however, because he was also the owner of the Athletics and therefore could not be fired. He managed his last game at the age of 87. He also lost 3,948 games for a winning percentage of .486. Mack did win nine AL pennants and five World Series (1910, 1911, 1913, 1929 and 1930) compared to five league pennants and two world championships for La Russa through 2009. Second is John McGraw with 2,763 wins for the Baltimore Orioles (1899, 1901–02) and New York Giants (1902–32). McGraw won ten NL pennants and three World Series. Taking only the period from 1914 through 2010 into consideration, La Russa ranks first in regular season wins.

Cardinals

25
October

On this date in 1987, the Cardinals lost game seven of the World Series 4-2 to the Twins in Minneapolis. Jim Lindeman and Steve Lake stroked RBI-singles in the second inning to give the Cards a 2-0 lead. The Twins came back, however, with single runs in the second and fifth off Joe Magrane, in the sixth against Danny Cox, and in the eighth off Todd Worrell. Over the last seven innings, only two St. Louis batters reached base. It was one of the most unusual World Series in history. The Cards had a 95-67 regular season record, while the Twins were only 85-77. Despite the 4-3 split in the seven-game series, the games themselves weren't particularly close. None was settled by less than a two-run margin, and the latest tie score of any of the seven contests was a 1-1 deadlock in the seventh inning of the third game. The home team won all seven games. The Twins were 4-0 in the Metrodome, scoring 33 runs, and 0-3 at Busch Stadium, with just five tallies. Counting the postseason, the Twins, aided by the deafening noise level inside the Metrodome, were 62-25 in Minneapolis and 31-57 elsewhere in 1987.

Cardinals

26

October

On the date in 1985, the Cardinals were three outs from the world championship before losing a controversial 2-1 decision to the Roy-als in Kansas City in game six of the World Series. The score was 0-0 after seven innings. Danny Cox of the Cards and Charlie Leibrandt of the Royals were pitching superbly. St. Louis broke through for a run in the eighth. After Terry Pendleton singled and Cesar Cedeno walked, pinch-hitter Brian Harper delivered a run-scoring single. The 1-0 margin remained until the ninth. With Todd Worrell on the mound, pinch-hitter Jorge Orta led off with a bouncer to first baseman Jack Clark. Clark tossed to Worrell, who was covering first. In an inexplicable call, umpire Don Denkinger ruled Orta safe. Television replays showed that not only did Worrell beat Orta to the base, but Orta stepped on the pitcher's foot. Frazzled by Denkinger's decision, the Cardinals made one mistake after another to lose the game. The next hit-ter, Steve Balboni, lifted a pop foul that Clark and catcher Darrell Porter let drop untouched in front of the dugout. Balboni singled to left. With one out, Worrell walked Hal McRae to load the bases. Pinch-hitter Dane Iorg, who played for the Cardinals from 1977 through 1984, arched a blooper into short right scoring the tying and winning runs.

Cardinals

**27
October**

Still seething over the game six loss the previous night, the Cardinals lost game seven of the World Series 11-0 in Kansas City on this date in 1985. It was over in a hurry as the Royals scored two runs in the second inning, three in the third, and six in the fifth. John Tudor, making his third start of the series, was relieved in the third. He angrily smashed an electric fan in the dugout and opened a gash in his left hand that required stitches. In the fateful fifth, the Cardinals used five pitchers. Joaquin Andujar and Whitey Herzog were both ejected for arguing the ball-and-strike calls of home plate Don Denkinger, who had blown the call at first base the previous evening. (Andujar was suspended for the first ten games of the 1986 season as a result of his tantrum, in which he bumped Denkinger twice.) Bret Saberhagen pitched the shutout. The name *Don Denkinger* is not one to utter in polite company near St. Louis, and many in Cardinal Nation blame him for the loss of the championship. But the Cardinals' anemic offense should shoulder much of the blame. The club scored only 13 runs in the seven games.

28
October

The question of the day: How did the Cardinals help end the "Curse of the Bambino?"

The Cardinals reached the World Series in 2004 and played the Boston Red Sox, who had staged a stunning comeback in which they beat the New York Yankees in the American League Championship Series after trailing three games to none. The Sox hadn't won a World Series since 1918. The "Curse of the Bambino" stemmed from the sale of Babe Ruth by the Red Sox to the Yankees in January 1920. The Yankees won 26 world championships from 1920 through 2000. The Cardinals contributed to the "curse" by beating the Red Sox in seven-game World Series in both 1946 and 1967. In 2004, Boston swept the Redbirds in four straight games by scores of 11-9, 6-2, 4-1 and 3-0. The Cardinals' starting pitchers in the Series were Woody Williams, Matt Morris, Jeff Suppan and Jason Marquis. They combined to allow 18 runs, all earned, in 17⅓ innings. At the plate, Jim Edmonds was 1-for-15, and Scott Rolen was hitless in 15 at-bats.

Cardinals

29
October

On this date in 1942, Branch Rickey resigned as vice-president of the Cardinals to take a position as president and general manager of the Brooklyn Dodgers. Rickey and majority owner Sam Breadon began their working relationship in 1920 and had built the Cardinals into a model franchise, but the two gradually developed a mutual resentment, in large part because they had vastly different political and moral outlooks. In addition, Breadon believed that Rickey received more credit for the Cardinals' success than he deserved and itched to prove that he could build a winning club without Rickey. Rickey felt that Breadon meddled too much in the club's affairs, and Breadon responded by making key decisions without consulting him. By 1942, a working relationship was no longer possible even after the club had won the World Series that year. Rickey had an opportunity to replace Larry MacPhail as the Dodgers' president and general manager. MacPhail, who had been an officer in the Army during World War I, left the club to help with the World War II effort as an assistant to the Secretary of State in Washington as a lieutenant colonel. MacPhail had worked under Rickey in the Cardinal organization running the club's farm system in Columbus during the early 1930s, and he arranged for Rickey to purchase a 25 percent interest in the Dodgers.

Cardinals

30
October

The question of the day: What happened to the Cardinals and Dodgers after Rickey switched organizations in 1942?

In Brooklyn, Rickey had much more freedom to operate the club by his own standards than he had in St. Louis. He expanded the Dodgers' farm system and built a club that won six NL pennants from 1947 through 1956. Most importantly, Rickey integrated the major leagues in 1947 with the signing of Jackie Robinson. With Rickey's move from St. Louis to Brooklyn, the Dodgers' gain was the Cardinals' loss. The Cards won pennants again in 1943, 1944 and 1946 and finished one game behind the Dodgers in 1949, but those titles were accomplished largely with players signed and developed under the Rickey regime. Once those players aged, replacements from the once fruitful farm system were no longer available, and the Cardinals went through a long period of mediocrity that lasted into the early 1960s. Stan Musial concluded each of his first four full seasons in the majors with World Series appearances, but he spent the last 17 seasons of his career without playing in the Fall Classic.

Cardinals

31
October

The question of the day: Who was Samuel Long?

Samuel Long was a St. Louis businessman who in 1934 was judged to be legally competent because he predicted the Cardinals would play in the World Series. Long was the 81-year-old president of a warehouse company who sought in probate court to have a guardianship imposed by his children removed so that he could run his own business. During the court proceedings, Long testified that with two weeks remaining in the 1934 season, he predicted the Cardinals would play in the Fall Classic even though they were four games out of first place. Long cited his baseball prophecy as proof of his mental alertness. The judge agreed, and Long was free to make his own decisions.

Cardinals

November

Cardinals

01
November

Today's trivia: Who holds the all-time Cardinals record for triples in a season?

First baseman Perry Werden holds the all-time Cardinals record for triples in a season with 29 in 1893. (*Two* gold stars for you if you got that one right.) That season, he had 22 doubles and only one home run. Werden had an unusual career. A native of St. Louis, he started out as a pitcher with the St. Louis Maroons in the Union Association in 1884 and had a record of 12-1. He never pitched in the majors again, and appeared in only three big league games from 1885 through 1889. He played for the Cards in 1892 and 1893. Despite his 29 triples, the club failed to bring him back in 1894. He played in the minors for the Minneapolis Millers in 1894 and clobbered 42 homers and added 45 more in 1895. Those were astonishing figures for the period. No one in the majors topped the 30-home run level until Babe Ruth belted 54 for the Yankees in 1920. Werden returned to the majors in 1897 and played in 133 games for the Louisville Colonels of the National League.

Cardinals

02
November

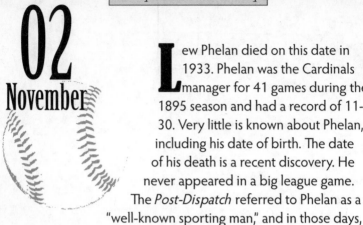

Lew Phelan died on this date in 1933. Phelan was the Cardinals manager for 41 games during the 1895 season and had a record of 11-30. Very little is known about Phelan, including his date of birth. The date of his death is a recent discovery. He never appeared in a big league game. The *Post-Dispatch* referred to Phelan as a "well-known sporting man," and in those days, a "sporting man" was a bookie. Phelan had been a partner in an Olive Street saloon the previous winter. "Just where he got his experience as a baseball manager is a mystery to the local fans," reported the St. Louis daily. Von der Ahe's mistress, Della Wells, was a relative of Phelan's, which probably explains the hiring. Phelan was fired before the season was over. Although not credited as such in the official record books, contemporary newspapers reported that Von der Ahe ran the club from the bench over the last weeks of the season, which resulted in a 39-92 record for the Cardinals.

Cardinals

03
~November

The question of the day: How did Mark McGwire help "save" base-ball in 1998?

Although his admission that he used performance-enhancing drugs has tainted his 70-home run season in 1998, Mark McGwire was credited by many at the time for "saving" baseball with the publicity surrounding his pursuit of the single-season home run record. The sport was still reeling from the strike that prematurely ended the 1994 season on August 12, and canceled the postseason, and delayed the beginning of the 1995 campaign until the final week of April. Through 1997, only two hitters had topped 60 home runs in the major leagues. Babe Ruth struck 60 home runs in 1927 and Roger Maris surpassed him with 61 in 1961. Maris stood almost unopposed as the single-season home run king for more than 30 years. Until 1996, his closest challengers were Willie Mays, with 52 for the Giants in 1965, George Foster, with 52 for the Reds in 1977, and Cecil Fielder, who clubbed 51 for the Tigers in 1990. Beginning in the 1990s, an offensive explosion gripped baseball that included an increase in home runs. McGwire belted 56 homers in 1996 for the Athletics and put up 58 in 1997 in a season split with the A's and the Cardinals.

Cardinals

04
November

The question of the day: When did the build-up for the pursuit of Maris's home run record begin in 1998?

Both Mark McGwire and Ken Griffey, Jr. of the Mariners were besieged with questions during spring training in 1998 about the possibility of breaking Maris's home run record. Griffey hit 56 homers in 1997. No one was mentioning Maris and Cubs outfielder Sammy Sosa in the same sentence. After all, Sosa's career high at that point was 40 in 1996. He had 36 in 1997. McGwire disappointed no one. On May 24, he had 24 homers in 48 games. On the same day, Sosa had nine homers in 39 games. Sosa then embarked on a home run streak unmatched in baseball history. From May 25 through June 25, he hit 25 homers in 29 games. In June alone, Sosa hit 20 homers, breaking the old mark for home runs in a month set by the Tigers' Rudy York, who had 18 in August 1937. Fans heaped adulation on both McGwire and Sosa as each plate appearance by the two sluggers was greeted with ovations. Sosa won the hearts of the people with his infectious enthusiasm and public insistence that McGwire was the man of the moment. McGwire, for his part, contended that Sosa deserved to win the League's MVP.

Cardinals

05
November

The question of the day: Where did McGwire and Sosa stand at the start of September in 1998?

McGwire and Sosa both finished August with 55 homers apiece, one short of Hack Wilson's NL record of 56, set with the Cubs in 1930. McGwire hit two home runs on September 1 to break Wilson's record and his 60th on September 5, tying Babe Ruth's 1927 standard in the Cardinals 142nd game. The Cardinals and Cubs met in a two-game series in St. Louis on September 7 and 8. Heading into the series, McGwire had 60 homers and Sosa 58. McGwire rose to the occasion by tying Maris with his 61st homer off Mike Morgan on September 7 and his 62nd a day later facing Steve Trachsel. In a postgame party on the field, McGwire was given a 1962 red Corvette. He and his son took a slow drive around the field as the crowd cheered. The drama was far from over, however, because there were 18 games left in the season. Even though McGwire broke Maris's 1961 mark, there was a possibility that Sosa could wind up as the all-time single-season record holder when the 1998 campaign ended.

06
November

The question of the day: What happened in 1998 after Mark McGwire hit his 62nd home run? Sammy Sosa tied McGwire by hitting his 62nd home run on September 13. McGwire struck number 63 on the 15th and Sammy tied him again a day later. McGwire hit number 64 on the 18th and 65 on the 20th. Sosa matched him again on the 23rd to reach 65, then passed McGwire with his 66th in the Astrodome off Jose Lima on September 25. Just 45 minutes later in Montreal, the lead evaporated when McGwire struck his 66th. It was the 21st time that the two homered on the same day. In the final two games of the season, McGwire hit four homers to finish the season with 70. Sosa remained stuck on 66. Ken Griffey, Jr. had a 56-home run season that would have created headlines in any year except 1998. McGwire's home run record would last only three years, however. Barry Bonds belted 73 home runs for the Giants in 2001.

Cardinals

07 November

Happy Birthday, Chris Von der Ahe, who was born on this date in 1851 in Germany. He owned the St. Louis franchise from its inception in 1882 until 1899. Easily the most colorful baseball owner of the 19th century, Von der Ahe never fully understood the game yet built a dynasty during the club's ten seasons in the American Association, winning four consecutive pennants beginning in 1885 and becoming a very wealthy man in the process. St. Louis was still one of the strongest teams in the AA when the organization folded after the 1891 season, moving to the National League, beginning with the 1892 season, where it immediately began serving as a doormat, a situation that helped bring Von der Ahe financial ruin. In his early years in St. Louis, he wasn't just a winner—he won with flair. His personal style incorporated checked slacks, spats, gaudy waistcoats, and diamond stickpins. Von der Ahe often brought his pet greyhounds to the games. He spoke in a thick German accent and referred to himself as Der Boss President. He also spent extravagantly. Among his indulgences was a sequence of very expensive and very public mistresses. He traveled in private trains and stayed in the most lavish hotels.

Cardinals

08
November

The question of the day: How did the dark side of Chris Von der Ahe surface?

On the negative side, Chris Von der Ahe had an abysmal knowledge of the finer points of the game. But he didn't let his ignorance stop him from constantly interfering with his managers. With the exception of Charlie Comiskey, who managed the club for six seasons and parts of two others and won all four American Association pennants, Von der Ahe hired and fired managers at a whim, sometimes employing as many as five in a single year. He imposed fines for routine errors and demanded that his players live in rooming houses he owned and drink only at the many saloons he operated around town. When the club played below his standards, he turned vindictive. After St. Louis lost the 1887 World Series to the National League champion Detroit Wolverines, Von der Ahe refused to pay his players for their work in the postseason. They lost the 1888 World Series to the New York Giants, and again Von der Ahe declined to pay his players. Only Comiskey's intervention defused a player revolt.

Cardinals

09
November

The question of the day: How did Chris Von der Ahe assemble the money to buy the Cardinals at the age of 30?

Little is known about Chris Von der Ahe's early life. He was born in Germany and came to the United States in 1867 at the age of 15, and like many immigrants, settled in New York. In 1870, he moved to St. Louis, where he worked as a grocery clerk and eventually owned a tavern called the Golden Lion Saloon at Grand and St. Louis Avenues in what then was a largely undeveloped part of the city. He bought real estate and increased his earnings as a landlord. His saloon was near Sportsman's Park, where large crowds attended games before heading to the Golden Lion. Von der Ahe became owner of the franchise we know today as the Cardinals in 1881 for $1,800. With a successful team, he turned a tidy profit. After games, flanked by two armed guards, he would ceremoniously cart the day's receipts in a wheelbarrow to the bank a block away.

Cardinals

10
November

The question of the day: How did Chris Von der Ahe's days as owner of the Cardinals come to an end?

The Cardinals began to unravel in the early 1890s with the club's move to the National League. When he was winning, Von der Ahe was viewed as an eccentric. With a losing team, his image was that of a buffoon. The end came in 1898, when Sportsman's Park burned down, his wife sued him for divorce because of infidelity, his mistress sued him for breach of promise, his son took him to court over a property matter, and he ended up in a Pittsburgh jail after Pirates owner William Nimick had him kidnapped by private detectives and shanghaied to Pennsylvania over a debt of $2,500. The NL agreed to pay the debt if Von der Ahe got out of baseball. Destroyed financially, he couldn't even sell his team because a Missouri court had appointed a receiver to dispose of it. The team was eventually sold at auction. Von der Ahe died nearly penniless from cirrhosis of the liver in 1913. On top of his gravesite at Bellefontaine Cemetery is a life-sized statue of Von der Ahe. In keeping with his outsized and eccentric personality, he had arranged for the adornment in 1885 when he was flush with cash.

Cardinals

**11
November**

On this date in 2001, Mark McGwire announced his retirement. Slowed by a bad knee, McGwire hit 29 homers in 299 at-bats in 2001, but batted only .187. McGwire had agreed to a $30 million, two-year contract extension in spring training that would cover the 2002 and 2003 seasons, but he never signed the deal. "After considerable discussion with those close to me," McGwire said, "I have decided not to sign the extension as I am unable to perform at a level equal to the salary the organization would be paying me. I believe I owe it to the Cardinals and the fans of St. Louis to step aside so a talented free agent can be brought in as the final piece of what I expect can be a world championship-caliber team." McGwire returned to the Cardinals as a hitting coach in 2010.

Cardinals

12
November

Today's trivia: Who ranks in the top ten in Cardinals history with the most at-bats without a home run?

Player	Years with the Cardinals	Position	At-bats
Hugh Nicol	1883–86	OF	1,488
Emil Verban	1944–46	2B	1,096
Gene Paulette	1917–19	1B	937
Shad Barry	1906–08	OF	799
Bill Doak	1913–24, 1929	P	775
Eddie Phelps	1909–10	C	576
Debs Garms	1943–45	OF	544
Larry Jackson	1955–62	P	538
Pickles Dillhoefer	1919–21	C	494
Howie Pollet	1941–43, 1946–51	P	489
Al Burch	1906–07	OF	489

Cardinals

13
November

Happy Birthday, Steve Bilko, who was born on this date in 1928. A first baseman, he stood six-foot-one and weighed between 230 and 260 pounds, depending on the stage of his latest diet. He played in 219 games as a Cardinal from 1949 through 1954 and hit .248 with 24 home runs in 778 at-bats. Bilko was hampered by the fluctuations in his weight, a tendency to strike out, and injuries. In 1952 he broke his arm when he tripped between first base and the dugout. He was dealt to the Cubs in 1954 and went down to the minors a year later. With the minor league Los Angeles Angels of the Pacific Coast League, he became a cult hero. From 1955 through 1957, he hit .330 with 148 home runs. The popular television character Sgt. Bilko played by Phil Silvers on *The Phil Silvers Show*, which aired from 1955 through 1959, and later in syndication, was named after Steve Bilko because he was series creator Nat Hiken's favorite player. Steve Martin portrayed Sgt. Bilko in the 1996 movie version of the series.

Cardinals

14
November

The question of the day: When did Tony La Russa first bat the pitcher in the eighth spot in the batting order?

La Russa began the practice of hitting the pitcher eighth on July 9, 1998. The Cardinal manager said the ploy "gives us a better shot to score runs. It's an extra guy on base in front of Ray (Lankford), Mark (McGwire) and Brian (Jordan). The more guys on base, the less they will be able to pitch around Mark." For the record, the 1998 Cardinals scored 4.98 runs per games with the pitcher batting ninth and 4.96 with the pitcher hitting eighth. It was not a one-year experiment. La Russa continues to use the strategy from time to time.

Cardinals

15
November

Billy Southworth died on this date in 1969. He managed the Cardinals in 1929 and again from 1940 through 1945. The Cardinals won the NL pennant in 1928, but fired manager Bill McKechnie after he lost the World Series to the Yankees. Southworth was hired to replace McKechnie, but was fired in July after a 43-45 start. The Cards kept Southworth in the organization as a minor league manager. While managing in the minors in 1932, his wife and twin babies died in childbirth. Already a heavy drinker, Southworth's alcohol consumption increased after the tragedy. A few years later, he gave up the booze and remarried a woman 19 years his junior in 1935. After winning several league championships in the minors, he was hired again by the Cardinals on June 7, 1940. The Cards won the NL pennant under Southworth in 1942, 1943 and 1944 and the World Series in 1942 and 1944. He would suffer another family catastrophe in 1945 when his son died during a routine training flight as a pilot during World War II. Billy Southworth, Jr. had previously survived 25 bombing runs over Europe.

Cardinals

16
November

On this date in 1932, 26-year-old Cardinals starting shortstop Charlie Gelbert shot himself in the leg in a hunting accident. Gelbert was hunting rabbits near McConnellsburg, Pennsylvania, when he tripped over a vine. In the process, his 12-gauge shotgun discharged and opened a nasty wound above his left ankle. Gelbert was unable to play during the 1933 and 1934 seasons while recovering. Nerves were severed, the instep blown away, gangrene set in, and three operations were performed to repair the damage caused by the blast. By the time he was healthy enough to return in 1935, his speed was gone and he lasted only two more seasons as a utility infielder. After his playing days ended, Gelbert was a coach at Lafayette College for 21 years.

Cardinals

17 November

Happy Birthday Pat Deasley. A catcher with the Cardinals in 1883 and 1884, Deasley was born in Ireland on this date in 1857. He was arrested on May 13, 1884, for drunkenness and making "insulting comments to ladies" during a spree in Indianapolis. He apparently propositioned to women, and when his overtures were rejected, Deasley grabbed one of the women by the arm. Both women escaped to the safety of a store that sold ladies' hats. Deasley pursued them, and the police arrived to arrest him. He was fined $20 in court the next day, but six days later he was seriously injured in a fight with teammates Tom Dolan and Joe Quest. The Cardinals asked Deasley's wife to join the team on future road trips to keep him in line. He was released at the end of the season. Deasley and Dolan feuded all season. Dolan was furious that Deasley was drawing a higher salary and receiving more playing time. Later in the season, Dolan hired a teammate to beat up Deasley so Dolan could be the first-string catcher. When that didn't work, Dolan jumped to the St. Louis Maroons in the Union Association.

Cardinals

18
November

Today's trivia: How many former Cardinals managers are in the Hall of Fame?

The Cardinals have had 12 managers who were subsequently elected to the Hall of Fame, although many were inducted for their roles as a player or front office executive. Those in the Hall of Fame, with the years they managed the Cardinals, are Charlie Comiskey (1885–89, 1891), Tommy McCarthy (1890), Roger Connor (1895), Roger Bresnahan (1909–12), Miller Huggins (1913–17), Branch Rickey (1919-25), Rogers Hornsby (1925–26), Bill McKechnie (1928–29), Frankie Frisch (1933–37), Billy Southworth (1940–45), Red Schoendienst (1965–76, 1980 and 1990) and Whitey Herzog (1980–90). Joe Torre (1990–95) and Tony La Russa (1996–present) are certain to be elected into the Hall of Fame in the future.

Cardinals

19
November

On this date in 1962, the Cardinals traded Don Cardwell and Julio Gotay to the Pirates for Dick Groat and Diomedes Olivo. The Cardinals had below average production at shortstop for nearly a decade before acquiring Groat, who was 32 and won the NL MVP award in 1960 as a Pirate. For short-term value, it was one of the best trades in Cardinals history. In his first two seasons in St. Louis, Groat made the NL All-Star team and rounded out an infield that included first baseman Bill White, second baseman Julian Javier and third baseman Ken Boyer. In 1963, Groat was the runner-up in the National League MVP balloting after hitting .318 with 201 hits and a league-leading 43 doubles. In the world championship season of 1964, Groat batted .292. As a collegian at Duke University, he was an All-American basketball player. Although only five-foot-eleven, he scored 831 points for Duke's 1951–52 basketball team, which was then the NCAA record. Groat played in 26 contests during the 1952–53 season with the Fort Wayne Pistons in the NBA and averaged 11.9 points per game.

Cardinals

20
November

The question of the day: How did pitching dominate the opening series of the 1943 season?

The Cardinals opened the 1943 season with four games against the Reds in Cincinnati from April 21 through April 24. The Reds won the first two games 1-0 in 11 innings and 1-0 again in ten. After starting the season with 26 consecutive scoreless innings, the Cards won the third game 2-1 with runs in the sixth and eighth innings. Stan Musial scored both runs, one on an error and one on a passed ball. The Cards won the fourth contest 1-0. The lone run crossed the plate in the fifth inning on a triple by Walker Cooper and a squeeze bunt from Buster Adams. It was the first RBI of the season for the Cards, and it came in the 35th inning of the season. The six runs in the four games was the result of an inferior batch of base-balls manufactured with different specifications due to shortages caused by World War II military priorities. A more resilient ball was soon rushed into use.

21
November

Happy Birthday, Stan Musial, who was born on this date in 1920 in Donora, Pennsylvania. Musial had the greatest day of his remarkable career on May 2, 1954, when he clubbed a major league record five home runs during a doubleheader against the New York Giants at Busch Stadium. In the first game, Musial hit three homers and drove in six runs during a 10-6 victory. Stan the Man hit a solo homer in the third inning and a two-run bomb in the fifth off Johnny Antonelli, as well as a three-run shot in the eighth against Jim Hearn to break a 6-6 tie. Wally Moon and Tom Alston also homered for the Cards. In the second tilt, Musial homered off Hoyt Wilhelm in the fifth and seventh innings, but the Cards lost 9-7. He also hit a 410-foot fly ball that Willie Mays caught in right-center. Musial is the only Cardinals player with five homers in consecutive games. The only other individual in major league history with five homers in a doubleheader is Nate Colbert of the Padres on August 1, 1972. A St. Louis native, Colbert was also at Busch Stadium on the day that Musial hit his five homers, sitting in the stands as an eight-year-old with his father.

Cardinals

22
November

The question of the day: What was the daffiest play in Cardinals history?

The play took place on June 30, 1959, when two balls were in play at the same time during a game against the Cubs at Wrigley Field. With the Cards batting in the fourth inning, the count was 3-1 on Musial with Bob Anderson pitching. Anderson's next pitch sailed past catcher Sammy Taylor entitling Stan Musial to first base on the walk. Taylor claimed the ball hit Musial's bat, and therefore he failed to pursue the ball as it rolled back to the screen. Taylor began arguing with home plate umpire Vic Delmore, and Chicago manager Bob Scheffing joined Taylor in the discussion. Musial rounded first base and headed for second. Third baseman Al Dark realized the ball was in play and ran full speed toward the backstop to get the ball. With Dark charging in, the batboy tossed the ball to field announcer Pat Pieper, who acted as though it were a hot potato and dropped it. Dark reached down, grabbed the ball, and threw it to shortstop Ernie Banks in an attempt to retire Musial (see November 23 for the rest of the story).

Cardinals

23
November

The question of the day: How did a second ball come into play during the bizarre play on June 30, 1959?

As Al Dark pegged his throw to Ernie Banks, umpire Vic Delmore gave Sammy Taylor a new ball as the two continued to argue. Bob Anderson, who was also arguing with the umpire, saw Musial race for second. Anderson grabbed the ball out of Taylor hands at almost the precise moment that Dark's throw was headed in the same direction. Banks fielded Dark's throw on one hop. Anderson's throw sailed into center field. While all this was happening Stan Musial slid safely into second. Musial saw Anderson's throw head into the outfield and started for third. But he hadn't taken more than two or three steps past second when Banks tagged him. Center fielder Bobby Thomson retrieved the second ball and lobbed it toward the Cubs dugout. The umpires huddled for ten minutes and ruled that Musial should return to first base. Scheffing protested, and the umps conferred again, this time calling Musial out. Cardinal manager Solly Hemus objected immediately, claiming interference by the batboy nullified the play. Hemus intended to file a formal protest with the National League office, but he never sent it because the Cardinals won 4-1.

Cardinals

24
November

The question of the day: What changes were made to the second Busch Stadium in 1996 and 1997? With the opening of the Edward Jones Dome for the Rams, football was no longer played at Busch Stadium, and changes were made to make the facility more conducive to baseball. Grass replaced the artificial turf in 1996. The Family Pavilion, featuring a variety of games and attractions, and Homer's Landing, a picnic area in left field, also opened. The predominant color scheme also changed from blue to green. In 1997, the Cardinals installed a hand-operated scoreboard 17 feet high and 270 feet wide and flag decks in the outfield's upper deck commemorating the team's World Series championships and retired uniform numbers. Capacity was reduced from 57,769 to 49,676. About 1,400 luxury seats were added. The bullpens were moved from foul territory to behind the fences in left and right.

25
November

On this date in 1947, Sam Breadon sold the Cardinals to a group headed by Fred Saigh and Robert Hannegan. Breadon had been majority owner since 1920, and under his stewardship, the Cardinals developed from a debt-ridden club into one of the most successful franchises in the game. By 1947, he was 71 years old and suffering from cancer. Breadon had seen the heirs of Colonel Jacob Ruppert forced into selling the New York Yankees to meet inheritance requirements, and he had no desire to inflict that responsibility on his wife, daughter and stepdaughters. Breadon also wanted to choose his own successors. He shopped the Cardinals quietly and found willing buyers in Hannegan, the US Postmaster General in Harry Tremens' administration, and Fred Saigh, local attorney and real estate investor. By putting up Saigh's downtown real estate holdings as collateral, Hannegan and Saigh managed to pay $4 million for the Cardinals with only $60,800 in cash. The rest was borrowed in a labyrinth of financial deals and what Saigh referred to a "tax gimmicks." The sale price was the highest in baseball history up to that point. Breadon didn't have long to enjoy his retirement, however. He died in May 1949.

26
November

The question of the day: Who was Fred Saigh?

At the time Fred Saigh and Robert Hannegan purchased the Cardinals in 1947, Saigh held 51 per cent of the stock. Hannegan held the other 49 per cent but was in ill health and died in October 1949 at the age of 46. The previous January, he sold his shares to Saigh for $1 million, which gave Saigh control of the franchise. The five-foot-five son of Syrian immigrants who had built a chain of groceries and small department stores in northern Illinois, Saigh became an accomplished tax and corporate attorney and accumulated a large fortune in real estate and stocks. Known as a financial wizard, he owned two entire blocks of valuable property in the heart of downtown St. Louis. He was 42 years old when he bought the club. Saigh owned the Cardinals until February 1953 when a conviction for tax evasion forced him to sell the club to August Busch. Saigh remained a devoted Cardinals fan until his death in 1996, but he refused to attend games in person because of his dislike of Busch.

Cardinals

**27
November**

On this date in 1956, Cardinals outfielder Charlie Peete died in a plane crash in Venezuela at the age of 27 along with his wife and three children. The plane on which they were traveling struck a fog-shrouded mountain peak near Caracas. Peete was en route to Caracas to play winter ball. He played in 23 games for the Cards in 1956 as a rookie after winning the American Association batting title at Omaha. The Cardinals had planned to make him the starting center fielder in 1957.

Cardinals

28
November

Today's trivia: What is Bob Gibson's overall record in the World Series?

Bob Gibson started three games in three World Series—against the Yankees in 1964, the Red Sox in 1967 and the Tigers in 1968. He had a record of 7-2, including three victories in 1967. The seven wins came in consecutive starts.

Gibson completed eight of his nine starts and had shutouts in both 1967 and 1968. In 81 innings, he allowed 55 hits, walked 17, struck out 91 and compiled an ERA of 1.89. Gibson was the winner of the seventh game in 1964 and 1967 to become the only pitcher in World Series history with two game seven victories. He is also the only pitcher to hit a home run in a game seven. It happened in 1967 off Jim Lonborg at Fenway Park. Gibson is one of two pitchers with two World Series homers. The second one was off Joe Sparma of the Tigers in game four in 1968. The other pitcher to accomplish the feat is Dave McNally of the Orioles in 1969 and 1970. No one else has a World Series home run and a ten-strikeout game on his resume. Gibson did it in both 1967 and 1968 in the same game.

Cardinals

29
November

Arlie Latham died on this date in 1952 at the age of 92. His baseball career lasted over 70 years. A third baseman, Latham played in St. Louis from 1883 through 1889 and was the sparkplug on four American Association championships. He was known for his enthusiasm, fielding acumen and base-stealing abilities. After his playing days ended, Latham became the first individual appointed specifically as a coach when the Reds hired him in 1900, and he later coached the New York Giants under John McGraw. Latham lived in England for 17 years during the 1910s and 1920s, promoting the American pastime as England's Administrator of Baseball. While there, he mingled with royalty and became friends with the Prince of Wales, who later became King George VIII. After returning to the States, Latham worked for both the Giants and the Yankees as a press box custodian at the Polo Grounds and Yankee Stadium, a position he enjoyed until his death.

Cardinals

30
November

Today's trivia: When was the coach's box created?

The American Association passed a new rule in 1887 that created the coach's box. It was passed with St. Louis in mind and was particularly directed at the antics of player-manager Charlie Comiskey, Arlie Latham and Bill Gleason. At the time, teams didn't hire full-time coaches. First and third base coaches were simply players who either weren't playing that day or were not batting during the inning. Comiskey, Latham and Gleason would chase the umpire around the field to be near enough to intimidate him on close calls. The Cardinal trio also ran onto the field to urge teammates around the bases. With his quick and sarcastic wit, Latham was particularly vicious in taunting umpires and opposing players who could be easily rattled. Latham would often edge near the grandstand to address the crowd. The "Arlie Show" was worth the price of admission as many fans came to the park solely to watch him torment the opposition and the umpires. If he had been born 100 years later, it's likely that Latham would have become famous as a stand-up comic or a television commentator. The creation of the coach's box helped to corral the Cardinals' players, but it failed to curb their tongues, and umpires and opposition players still received an earful.

Cardinals

December

Cardinals

01
December

The question of the day: How did bringing in the fences at Robison Field in 1909 reduce the number of home runs hit at the ballpark?

The changes reduced the home run distance from 470 feet to 380 in left field, 520 to 400 in left-center, 500 feet to 435 in straightaway center and 290 to 280 in right field. The peculiar angle of the field, with a gargantuan left field and a short right field, was necessary because of the lot's restrictive rectangular shape at the corner of Natural Bridge and Vandeveter. Due to the reverse logic of the dead ball era, the shorter fences turned Robison Field from an above-average home run park to one that was below the NL average. During the period, a drive of 350 feet was noteworthy. Most home runs were inside-the-park, splitting the gaps between the outfielders and rolling to the fences. The new shorter fences erected in 1909 at Robison Field stopped many of those drives, and what had formerly been inside-the-park homers became triples and doubles.

Cardinals

02 December

Happy Birthday, Darryl Kile, who was born on this date in 1968. On June 22, 2002, Kile was found dead at the team hotel in Chicago. He was survived by his wife, Flynn, his five-year-old twins (son Kannon and daughter Sierra) and a ten-month-old son, Ryker. At 12:25 p.m., a little more than two hours before game time at Wrigley Field, several Cardinals realized that Kile wasn't at the ballpark and called the Westin Hotel and asked to check on him. The hotel security director and maintenance man went to Kile's suite. The pitcher was found in his bed. Police estimated that Kile had been dead for eight to ten hours. The game against the Cubs was postponed. Kile showed no health problems during a routine physical in spring training, although he complained of shoulder pain and weakness the night before he died. He had no history of heart problems and was not on medication, but his father died of a heart attack in his mid-40s in 1993. An autopsy revealed he likely died from blocked coronary arteries. Kile's sudden death came only four days after the passing of longtime broadcaster Jack Buck at the age of 77.

Cardinals

03
December

On this date in 1901, the American League transferred the Milwaukee Brewers to St. Louis. The new club in St. Louis was owned by Robert Hedges, who took the Cardinals' former nickname, former playing field, and many of the club's top players by the start of the 1902 season. Hedges named his club the Browns and signed a lease to play at Sportsman's Park at Grand and Dozier, where the Cardinals played from 1881 through 1892. There, Hedges built a new grandstand. He then went to work on recruiting the Cardinals' best players for his club. He was enormously successful. Jesse Burkett, Jack Harper, Emmett Hendrick, Jack Powell, Willie Sudhoff and Bobby Wallace all signed with the Browns. Harper, Powell and Sudhoff were the three best pitchers on the Cards in 1901, combining for 59 of the team's 76 victories in 1901. Burkett, a left fielder, batted .376, and Wallace, a shortstop, was the Cards' leading run producer with 91 RBIs. Padden was the starting second baseman and Heidrick the center fielder. Combined with the six players who moved to the AL between the 1900 and 1901 seasons (Cy Young, John McGraw, Wilbert Robinson, Lou Criger, Mike Donlin and Bill Keister), the Cardinals lost 14 players in two years, five of whom would eventually reach the Hall of Fame.

04 December

The question of the day: How did the creation of the American League and the Browns affect the Cardinals?

Among the regulars from the 1900 season, only outfielder Patsy Donovan was still with the Cards in 1902. It took years for the club to recover from the blow. The Cards, who had a 76-64 record in 1901, slumped to 56-78 in 1902 and 43-94 in 1903. The Browns, with a roster full of ex-Cardinals, landed in second place in 1902. From 1902 through 1920, the Cardinals had only three winning seasons, never finished higher than third place, or within 13 games of the pennant-winner.

05
December

On this date in 1957, the Cardinals traded Willard Schmidt, Marty Kutyna and Ted Wieand to the Reds for Curt Flood and Joe Taylor. This proved to be one of the greatest trades in Cardinals history. In exchange for three pitchers of little or no value, the Cardinals acquired Flood, who played center field for the club in 12 seasons and three World Series. At the time of the trade, Flood was only 19 years old and had four major league plate appearances. With 1,738 games as a Cardinal, Flood ranks sixth on the club's all-time list behind Hall of Famers Stan Musial, Lou Brock, Ozzie Smith, Enos Slaughter and Red Schoendienst.

Cardinals

06
December

Burleigh Grimes died on this date in 1985. Grimes was the winning pitcher for the Cardinals in game seven of the 1931 World Series, pitching 8⅔ innings of a 4-2 win over the Philadelphia Athletics at Sportsman's Park. George Watkins was the hitting star. He contributed to a two-run first inning with a single and hit a two-run homer in the third over the right field pavilion. Grimes took a 4-0 lead into the ninth before running into trouble. With two outs and a runner on first, he allowed a walk and a single to score two runs. Wild Bill Hallahan came in from the bullpen and retired Max Bishop on a fly ball to Pepper Martin in center field. The pivotal contest drew only 20,805, about 19,000 fewer than the 39,401 fans who attended game six. Tickets for the games in St. Louis were sold in three-game strips with the seventh game omitted. Game seven tickets didn't go on sale until after the sixth game ended, resulting in a diminished crowd. Grimes compiled a 30-15 record pitching for the Cardinals in 1930 and '31. He returned briefly in 1933 but at 39 years old his skills were gone.

Cardinals

07
December

The question of the day: How many one-hitters did Bill Doak pitch during his career?

Bill Doak pitched three one-hitters while with the Cardinals, and on each occasion the hit happened when he failed to reach first base in time to cover the bag on an infield hit. The first was on August 10, 1920, when he beat the Phillies 5-1 in Philadelphia. In the seventh inning, Cy Williams hit a ball that eluded first baseman Jack Fournier, moving to his right, but was fielded cleanly by second baseman Rogers Hornsby. Hornsby had plenty of time to throw out Williams, but Doak was late covering the bag and Williams was safe with a single. On May 11, 1922, Doak beat the Giants 2-0 in St. Louis. The lone New York hit was an infield single by Dave Bancroft leading off the first inning in which Doak was tardy reaching first base for the putout. On July 13, 1922, Doak's one-hitter beat the Phillies 1-0 in St. Louis. The only Philadelphia hit was an infield tapper by Curt Walker that was fielded by Fournier. Again, Doak failed to get to first base on time and Walker was safe.

Cardinals

08
December

O n this date in 1966, the Cardinals traded Charley Smith to the Yankees for Roger Maris. Maris became a living legend in 1961 when he hit 61 homers for the Yankees to break Babe Ruth's single-season record of 60 set in 1927. Maris also won the second of two consecutive MVP awards in 1961. He went into a slow decline after 1961, however, largely due to injuries. The Yankees traded Maris to the Cardinals after he hit only .233 with 13 homers and 43 RBIs in 1966. The Yankees had questioned his courage and dedication for complaining constantly about a sore hand. It was only after the trade that he found out he'd played most of the season with a broken hand, which the Yankee doctors had been unable to diagnose. Maris lasted two seasons in St. Louis before retiring at the age of 34. Injuries had diminished his skills. He hit only .258 with 12 homers in 720 at-bats as a Cardinal, but he played in five World Series as a Yankee and he knew what it took to win. With his quiet leadership and professionalism, Maris was a useful member of two pennant-winning teams in St. Louis. A grateful August Busch set up Maris with a beer distributorship after he retired.

Cardinals

09
December

The question of the day: What was Whitey Herzog's assessment of the Cardinals following his first season as manager in 1980?

"I've never seen such a bunch of misfits," Herzog said to August Busch. "Nobody would run out a ball. Nobody in the bullpen wanted the ball." Herzog was appalled not only by the lack of hustle and self-discipline, but also by the blatant drug use and the rampant egos. "You've got a bunch of mean people, some very sorry human beings," Herzog told Busch. "It's the first time I've ever been afraid to walk through my own clubhouse." In a span of five days beginning on December 8, Herzog remade the Cards starting with a trade of Terry Kennedy, Steve Swisher, John Littlefield, John Urrea, Mike Phillips, Kim Seaman and Alan Olmstead to the Padres for Rollie Fingers, Gene Tenace, Bob Shirley and Bob Geren. A day later, the Cards dealt Leon Durham, Ken Reitz and Tye Waller to the Cubs for Bruce Sutter. On December 12, Fingers went to the Brewers along with Ted Simmons and Pete Vuckovich for Sixto Lezcano, David Green, Lary Sorensen and Dave LaPoint.

Cardinals

10
December

On this date in 1981, the Cardinals traded Garry Templeton, Sixto Lezcano and Luis DeLeon to the Padres for Ozzie Smith, Steve Mura and Alan Olmstead. The trade wasn't officially completed until February 11, 1982, when Smith's and Templeton's contracts were worked out. The deal was a huge gamble for the Cardinals, but it paid off. Templeton looked like a future Hall of Famer in December 1981, but his questionable defense, work ethic, immaturity and behavioral problems earned him a ticket out of town. Templeton was a starter in San Diego for nine years but never put up the batting numbers that he had posted in St. Louis. Arguably the greatest defensive shortstop in baseball history, Smith earned a plaque in Cooperstown. Although weak with the bat early in his career, Smith built himself into a contributor on offense. From 1985 through 1993, he hit .281 with a .359 on-base percentage and an average of 36 stolen bases per season. He started in 12 All-Star Games and won 13 Gold Gloves. As a Cardinal, Smith ranks third in games played with 1,990, trailing only Stan Musial and Lou Brock. He is also sixth in hits (1,944), eighth in doubles (338) and third in steals (433).

11
December

The question of the day: How did the Cardinals win the 1934 pennant?

On September 4, there seemed to be little chance that the Cardinals would advance to the World Series. The New York Giants held a seven-game lead with 25 contests left on the schedule. The Cards were tied for second with the Cubs. But St. Louis would win 20 of their last 25 games to finish first despite a bone-wearying road trip. From August 31 through September 24, the Cards played 23 consecutive road games in which they visited each of the seven opposing ballparks, including Wrigley Field twice. The pitching staff was remarkable, allowing nine runs in a seven-game stretch beginning on September 13. Paul Dean threw a 12-inning shutout against the Giants and a no-hitter against the Dodgers. Dizzy Dean and Bill Walker also spun shutouts. Going into the final two days, the Cardinals and Giants were tied for first place. The Cardinals clinched the pennant when Paul Dean beat the Reds 6-1 in St. Louis on September 29 while Dizzy whitewashed Cincinnati 9-0 the following day. The Giants lost their final two games to their archrival Dodgers 5-1 and 8-5 at the Polo Grounds in New York.

Cardinals

12 December

On this date in 1903, the Cardinals traded Three Finger Brown and Jack O'Neill to the Cubs for Jack Taylor and Larry McLean. This trade proved to be one of the worst in Cardinals history. At the time of the transaction, Mordecai "Three Finger" Brown was 27 years old and had won only nine major league games. Once in Chicago, he became one of the best pitchers of his generation. He played in the majors for 13 more seasons and posted a record of 230-117 and an ERA of 2.56. He was elected to the Hall of Fame in 1949. Brown's nickname was the result of an accident he suffered at the age of seven while visiting his uncle's farm in Indiana. Brown stuck his right hand into a corn chopper and half the right index finger was shorn off. The thumb and middle finger were also badly damaged. As it healed, each finger twisted and bent unnaturally. The disfigured hand helped Brown in his pitching and it gave the ball a unique spin. Jack Taylor was 29 at the time of the trade and had records of 23-11 in 1902 and 21-14 in 1903 for the Cubs. He provided the Cardinals with one good season. In 1904, Taylor was 20-19 with an ERA of 2.22 in 352 innings and completed each of his 39 starts. After struggling through the next year, Taylor went back to the Cubs, with whom he discovered his winning ways.

Cardinals

13
December

On this date in 1934, the Cardinals sold Johnny Mize to the Reds for $55,000. The Reds acquired Mize on a conditional basis. He played well enough for the Reds during spring training to win the starting first base job, but doctors determined that a groin injury would require surgery and put him out of action for months. Leery of investing in "damaged goods," the Reds returned his contract to St. Louis. The Cardinals were extremely fortunate that the Reds passed on Mize. After the operation, he began playing in mid-season with the Cardinals' farm club in Rochester. A future Hall of Famer and one of the greatest sluggers ever to wear a Cardinals' uniform, Mize played for St. Louis from 1936 through 1941, compiling a batting average of .336, an on-base percentage of .419, and a slugging percentage of .600. He clubbed 158 homers while in a St. Louis uniform before a trade to the Giants on December 11, 1941. Mize remained in the majors until 1953 and hit 359 home runs despite missing three full seasons during World War II.

14
December

The question of the day: What were the circumstances surrounding Mark McGwire's 61st home run in 1998?

In the pre-game press conference prior to the Cardinals-Cubs match-up at Busch Stadium on September 7, McGwire and Sammy Sosa swapped one-liners and seemed to enjoy every minute of the media attention surrounding their race for the home run record. Entering the contest, McGwire had 60 homers and Sosa 58. During the game, McGwire hit his 61st home run in the first inning of the 3-2 Cardinals win. The drive was struck off Mike Morgan and carried 430 feet to the left field. The ball hooked to the left but curled inside the foul pole, ricocheted off one of the windows on the Stadium Club, and fell into section 281. As he crossed the plate, McGwire hugged his 10-year-old son Matthew, who arrived 30 minutes before game time. Also in attendance were Mark's parents. His father, John, was celebrating his 61st birthday on the day Mark hit his 61st homer. Five of the six children of the late Roger Maris were also in the stands. Their mother was hospitalized with a "heart flutter." After hitting the homer, McGwire saluted in the direction of the Maris family.

Cardinals

15
December

The question of the day: What were the circumstances surrounding Mark McGwire's 62nd home run in 1998?

McGwire's 62nd home run of 1998 was a blast off Steve Trachsel of the Cubs in the fourth inning of a 6-1 win on September 8 in St. Louis. The homer was a line drive that began to sink as it neared the eight-foot-high fence. The ball made it by less than two inches. At 341 feet, it was McGwire's shortest home run of the season and touched off an emotional celebration, not just in St. Louis, but around the country as the contest was broadcast on national television. In a daze, McGwire missed first base and was headed toward second before coach Dave McKay reminded him that he had neglected to touch the bag. Rounding the bases slowly while savoring every second, McGwire shook hands with Cubs infielders and catcher Scott Servais. At home plate, McGwire was hugged by Sammy Sosa, who had sprinted in from right field. McGwire also hugged his son Matthew and went to the front row of the stands to embrace the Maris family, which included all six children and his widowed wife.. The ball was picked up by groundskeeper Tim Forneris, who later gave it to McGwire.

Cardinals

16
December

The question of the day: How did a fan cost Mark McGwire a home run in 1998?

McGwire's home run total reached 65 during an 11-6 win over the Brewers in Milwaukee on September 20 with a first-inning blast off Scott Karl. In the fifth inning, facing Rod Hendrickson, who was making his major league debut, McGwire lost another potential home run when a fan appeared to interfere with a drive into the center field bleachers. In a controversial decision, second base umpire Bob Davidson ruled that the fan had reached over the wall, and McGwire was credited with a ground rule double. The fan thought to have touched the ball was Michael Chopps, a 31-year-old gym teacher from Waterford, Wisconsin, who was ejected from the stadium and fined $518 for trespassing. Replays showed that two fans, standing along the railing in front of the seats, had indeed reached out but never made contact with the ball until it passed the fence and fell into a gap between the padded wall and the outfield seats.

Cardinals

17
December

On this date in 1932, the Cardinals traded Jim Bottomley to the Reds for Estel Crabtree and Ownie Carroll. Bottomley shares the major league record for most runs-batted-in in a game with 12. The only other player to accomplish the feat is Mark Whitten of the Cardinals on September 7, 1993. Bottomley drove in an even dozen on September 16, 1924, during a 17-3 thrashing of the Dodgers at Ebbets Field. He also had six hits in six at-bats. In the first inning, Bottomley connected for a two-run single off Rube Ehrhardt. In the second, Bottomley had a run-scoring double against Bonnie Hollingsworth. Art Decatur gave up a grand slam to Bottomley in the fourth and a two-run homer in the sixth. The Cardinal first baseman had a two-run single against Tex Wilson in the seventh for his 10th and 11th RBIs. The record-breaking 12th RBI came on a single facing Jim Roberts in the ninth. Bottomley had another six-hit game on August 5, 1931, during a 16-2 victory over the Pirates in the second game of a doubleheader in Pittsburgh. The only other players with two six-hit games in a career are Cal McVey (both in 1876), Jimmie Foxx (1930 and 1932) and Kirby Puckett (1987 and 1991).

Cardinals

18 December

The question of the day: How did Stan Musial become an outfielder? Musial made a spectacular rise through the Cardinals' farm system after he was signed out of high school in Donora, Pennsylvania, in 1938. With Daytona Beach in the Florida State League in 1940, he played in 113 games, splitting his time between pitching and the outfield and compiling a record of 18-4 and a 3.13 ERA. An arm injury during spring training in 1941 ended his career as a pitcher. Musial made his major league debut on September 17, 1941, and hit .426 in 47 at-bats in a late-season trial. He leads the Cardinals in almost every offensive category. Among major league hitters, Musial ranks sixth in games played (3,036), ninth in at-bats (10,972), eighth in runs (1,949), fourth in hits (3,630), third in doubles (725), second in total bases (6,134), second in extra base hits (1,377) and fourth in RBIs (1,951). The only other players with at least 1,900 runs and 1,900 RBIs are Hank Aaron, Barry Bonds, Ty Cobb, Willie Mays and Babe Ruth. In addition, Musial hit 475 homers and compiled a .331 batting average. The only players with more homers and a higher batting average are Ruth, Lou Gehrig and Ted Williams.

Cardinals

19
December

Happy Birthday, Tom Lawless, who was born on this date in 1956. Lawless had a career batting average of .207 with only two homers and 24 RBIs over 531 at-bats between 1982 and 1990. Playing on the pennant-winning Cardinals in 1987, Lawless batted just 25 times during the regular season and had only two hits for an .080 batting average with a big fat zero in the RBI column. Due to an injury to Terry Pendleton, Lawless played three games during the 1987 World Series against the Twins in a platoon with Jose Oquendo. Lawless had only one hit in ten at-bats in the Series, but the hit was a three-run homer off Frank Viola in game four in St. Louis. The blast broke a 1-1 tie in the fourth inning of a game won by the Cardinals 7-2. Doing his best Reggie Jackson impersonation, Lawless stood at the plate to watch his drive sail toward the outfield and flipped his bat in the air when the ball cleared the fence. Lawless's only two regular season homers came in 1984 with the Reds and in 1988 with the Cardinals.

Cardinals

20
December

In a trade of superstar second base-men at the top of their game, the Cardinals dealt player-manager Rogers Hornsby to the Giants for Frankie Frisch on this date in 1926. The Giants also sent pitcher Jimmy Ring to the Cards in the transaction. The trade was completed a little over two months after the Cardinals won the World Series. Hornsby was never shy about expressing his opinion and didn't hesitate to crudely and tactlessly criticize Cards owner Sam Breadon when he disagreed with team policies. Hornsby wanted a three-year contract, while Breadon was offering only a one-year deal, although at $50,000, he would be the highest-paid player in baseball behind Babe Ruth. Breadon also wanted Hornsby to stop betting on horse racing, but Hornsby refused. (A year later, Hornsby was sued by a Newport, Kentucky, bookmaker, who claimed Hornsby owed him $92,000 in gambling debts. The case was settled out of court.) An off-year by Hornsby with the bat was another influence in the trade. After batting .403 in 1925, he fell to .317 in 1926 and Breadon was convinced he was slowing down. It was a gutsy move by Breadon to trade the best player in club history, and a man who had just taken the Cardinals to a world championship.

Cardinals

21
December

The question of the day: How did Cardinals fans react to the trade of Hornsby?

Cardinals fans were up in arms over the exile of Hornsby. Mayor Victor Miller and the St. Louis Chamber of Commerce contacted baseball commissioner Kenesaw Landis and National League president John Heydler to see if the trade could be canceled. Mark Steinberg, a member of the Cardinals board of directors, called the trade an "insult" to St. Louis fans. At a downtown intersection, an irate fan jumped on the running board of Sam Breadon's Pierce-Arrow and shouted insults until police chased him away. Breadon received so many abusive calls to his home that he disconnected his phone. His home and auto agency were festooned with black crepe by angry fans. One sportswriter vowed he would never cover another Cardinals game and kept the pledge for ten years. When the 1927 season started, fans at Sportsman's Park chanted "We Want Hornsby" repeatedly whenever Frisch stepped to the plate.

Cardinals

22
December

The question of the day: How did the Hornsby-for-Frisch trade pan out?

In the years that Frankie Frisch was the Cardinals starting second baseman, the club won pennants in 1928, 1930, 1931 and 1934. He also managed the Cards in 1934. Hornsby still had three great years ahead of him. From 1927 through 1929 he hit .376 with 86 homers, but he did it for three different teams as his prickly personality led to trades from the Giants to the Braves in 1928 and the Braves to the Cubs in 1929. Hornsby later managed the Braves (1928), Cubs (1930–32), Browns (1933–37 and 1952) and Reds (1952–53). He never managed another club in the World Series, although he played in one with the Cubs in 1929. Frisch was still a productive player well into the 1930s at a time when Hornsby was benched because of injuries. Ultimately, the Cardinals got the better of the deal, and the highly competitive Frisch won the hearts of the Cardinals fans. He played in 1,311 games for the club. He appeared in eight World Series (four with the Giants and four with the Cardinals), which is the most of any National Leaguer in history.

Cardinals

23
December

The question of the day: How did the Japanese attack on Pearl Harbor ruin the plans of Browns owner Donald Barnes and Cardinals owner Sam Breadon?

The attack on Pearl Harbor on December 7, 1941, prevented a possible move of the St. Louis Browns to Los Angeles. With a contending team, the Cardinals boosted their attendance from 324,078 in 1940 to 633,345 in 1941. The Browns, meanwhile, dropped from 239,591 in 1940 to 176,240 in 1941 despite winning 70 games for the first time since 1929. St. Louis had long been considered to be big enough for only one successful club, but neither the Cardinals nor the Browns would leave town. Despairing of ever turning a profit, Barnes finally set his sights on Los Angeles. At the time, no major league franchise had changed cities since 1903, and there was no big league club west of St. Louis. Barnes reached an agreement with Breadon in which Breadon would pay Barnes $350,000 for the exclusive rights to the St. Louis market. Barnes planned to use the loot to negotiate the purchase of the Los Angeles Angels, a minor league franchise in the Pacific Coast League owned by Cubs owned P. K. Wrigley.

Cardinals

24
December

The question of the day: Why was moving the Browns to Los Angeles impractical and unlikely.

The Los Angeles Browns would have played at Wrigley Field, a facility built in 1925 and a smaller (capacity 22,000) version of Wrigley Field in Chicago. The distance from Los Angeles to other American League cities, the nearest being Chicago, posed a problem. Teams in 1941 traveled exclusively by train, and a train from Chicago to Los Angles took two days, which would disrupt the playing schedule. Barnes made arrangements with Trans World Airlines to fly two ballplayers on each of the 21 daily flights from Chicago to L.A. to avoid the loss of an entire ball club to a crash. The plan was impractical, however, and illuminated the prevailing notion of the period that airplanes were dangerous. The proposal was supposed to come to a vote of American League owners on December 8, 1941, but Pearl Harbor changed all of that as the war put the immediate future of baseball into doubt.

Cardinals

25
December

The question of the day: Why didn't the Browns move immediately after World War II ended in 1945?

Before the war ended, Donald Barnes sold most of his stock in the Browns to Richard Muckerman. Also, an American League pennant in 1944, a season in which the Browns outdrew the Cardinals, convinced the new Browns owners the delusion that they could compete with their National League intra-city rivals. Muckerman, Bill DeWitt and Bill Veeck, who followed Barnes as owners of the Browns in the postwar period, decided to remain in St. Louis and continue to fight what became an increasingly futile battle with the Cardinals over fan patronage. The Browns would stay in St. Louis until September 1953 when the franchise moved to Baltimore and was renamed the Orioles. Los Angeles would not gain a major league team until the Dodgers moved from Brooklyn in October 1957.

Cardinals

26
December

Today's trivia: Who hit the first pinch-hit grand slam in major league history?

Cardinals pitcher Mike O'Neill hit the first pinch-hit grand slam in major league history on June 3, 1902, during an 11-9 win over the Braves in Boston. The Cardinals trailed the Braves 8-5 heading into the ninth inning. O'Neill's drive was inside-the-park and put St. Louis into the lead with his grand slam. O'Neill was primarily a pitcher but was often used as a pinch-hitter and occasionally as an outfielder. During his five-year career, he had a 34-43 record and hit .255 with nine homers in 380 at-bats. He was one of four brothers who played in the majors. The four O'Neill brothers were Jack (born in 1873), Mike (1877), Steve (1891) and Jim (1983). The oldest two brothers were born in Maam, Ireland, and the youngest two in the coal-mining town of Minooka, Pennsylvania. Jack, who was a catcher, was Mike's teammate with the Cardinals in 1902 and 1903. Steve had a long career in baseball. He was manager of the Indians, Tigers, Red Sox and Phillies between 1835 and 1954, and managed the Tigers to the AL pennant in 1945.

Cardinals

27
December

Happy Birthday, Byron Browne, who was born on this date in 1942. He was one of seven players involved in one of the most pivotal trades in baseball history. On October 7, 1969, the Cardinals traded Curt Flood, Tim McCarver, Joe Hoerner and Browne to the Phillies for Dick Allen, Cookie Rojas and Jerry Johnson. Flood refused to go to Philadelphia and filed a lawsuit against Major League Baseball to be declared a free agent. At the time, there was no free agency, as the reserve clause, which was created in 1879, kept every player in professional baseball bound to one club for life. Flood was 32, had been with the Cardinals for 12 years, and had no desire to move to the Phillies, then a losing club with a reputation as a difficult place for African-Americans to play. He first asked commissioner Bowie Kuhn to be declared a free agent, and he was denied. Flood filed the suit on January 16, 1970, stating that baseball had violated the nation's antitrust laws. Even though he was making $90,000, one of the top salaries in baseball at the start of the 1970s, Flood likened "being owned" to "being a slave 100 years ago."

Cardinals

28 December

The question of the day: What was the result of Curt Flood's lawsuit? Former Supreme Court Justice Arthur Goldberg argued Flood's case. Flood asked for changes in baseball's reserve clause and $1.4 million in damages. Goldberg agreed to work for expenses, which were paid by the Major League Players' Association. Flood's request for free agency was denied by the US District Court in New York and the Court of Appeals before the United States Supreme Court agreed to hear Flood's arguments. The ruling of the highest court in the land, which was rendered in June 1972, favored organized baseball in a 5-3 decision. Meanwhile, Flood sat out the 1970 season, but he signed with the Washington Senators in 1971 for $110,000. He played only 13 games for Washington and retired. The suit likely cost Flood several years of his career and hundreds of thousands of dollars. Although Flood lost the battle, the players won the war. Flood's suit paved the way for free agency, which started in 1976, and multi-million-dollar salaries.

Cardinals

29
December

The question of the day: Who was Vern Rapp?

Vern Rapp was one of the most controversial managers in Cardinals history. He was hired on October 7, 1976, to replace Red Schoendienst, who had guided the club for 12 seasons. Rapp's 179-game reign was one of almost constant turmoil. A graduate of Cleveland High School in St. Louis, Rapp never reached the majors as a player and was a manager in the minors as early as 1955 when he was only 27. He worked in the Yankees, Cardinals, Reds and Expos chains and had a long series of success. August Busch believed the Cardinals needed a disciplinarian in contrast to the laid-back attitude of Schoendienst. Rapp ran the Reds top farm team in Indianapolis from 1969 through 1975 and helped develop players who would contribute to four pennant winners and two world championships. The Reds were the most conservative organization in baseball with a policy of no mustaches or beards and strict rules about hair and sideburn length. There was also a rigid dress code both on and off the field.

Cardinals

30 December

The question of the day: How did Vern Rapp fare as manager of the Cardinals?

Rapp believed that a well-groomed player was a disciplined player and that the grooming rules were the fabric of a winning team. He wanted to enforce the same regulations in St. Louis that had been enforced in the Cincinnati Reds organization, a notion August Busch fervently supported. Players were less than enthusiastic about the idea, particularly Bake McBride, who had to shave off his mutton-chop sideburns, and Al Hrabosky, who believed that his Fu Manchu was part of his pitching arsenal. In Rapp's first year, the Cardinals were 83-79, an 11-game improvement over 1976, but he managed to alienate almost every athlete on the team in the process. Rapp was fired 17 games into the 1978 season with the club holding a 6-11 record. During spring training, he had well-publicized shouting matches with players Garry Templeton and Buddy Schultz. Shortly after the regular season began, Rapp called All-Star catcher Ted Simmons a "loser." The Cardinals hired Ken Boyer to replace Rapp. The 1978 Cardinals lost 93 games, the most of any team between 1924 and the present.

Cardinals

31
December

The question of the day: If one were construct an all-time Cardinals team of 25 players, with only the player's years with the club since 1900 taken into consideration, how would the "roster" be constructed?

The ten best pitchers in Cardinals history since 1900 are Bob Gibson, Dizzy Dean, Jesse Haines, Harry Brecheen, Bill Sherdel, Bill Doak, Bob Forsch, Mort Cooper, Max Lanier and Howie Pollet. The "starting line-up" would consist of Ted Simmons (C), Albert Pujols (1B), Rogers Hornsby (2B), Ken Boyer (3B), Ozzie Smith (SS), Lou Brock (LF), Stan Musial (CF), Enos Slaughter (RF) and Gibson (P). Musial was shifted to center, where he played 325 career games, to get three future Hall of Famers into the "line-up." The "bench" would consist of Curt Flood (OF), Joe Medwick (OF), Ray Lankford (OF), Jim Bottomley (1B), Red Schoendienst (2B), Marty Marion (SS) and Tim McCarver (C). The best players left off the "team" are Jim Edmonds (OF), Frankie Frisch (2B), Johnny Mize (1B), Willie McGee (OF) and Keith Hernandez (1B). Mark McGwire's time with the Cardinals (545 games) was too short for consideration.

Cardinals